The

TEMPEH

Cookbook

Dorothy R. Bates

BOOK PUBLISHING COMPANY

Food Stylist and Design: Eleanor Dale Evans

Photography: Thomas Johns

On the front cover, counter-clockwise from top: Mock Tuna Salad, pg.22, Spinach Mushroom Salad, pg.26, Hot German Potato Salad, pg. 28

On the back cover: Egg Rolls, pg. 14, Four Star Mince Pie, pg. 93

ISBN 0-913990-65-5

© 1989 Dorothy R. Bates

99 98 97   4 5 6

Bates, Dorothy R.
        The tempeh cookbook / by Dorothy R. Bates
                p.   cm.
        Includes index.
        ISBN 0-913990-65-5 : $10.95
        1. Cookery (Tempeh)   I. Title.   II. Tempeh cook book.
    TX814.5.T45B38   1989
    641.6'5655--dc20   89-35499
                                                            CIP

The Book Publishing Company
P.O. Box 99
Summertown, TN 38483

Table of Contents

Sandwiches

Main Dishes

Oriental

Italian

Mexican

American

International

Dessert

Introduction to Tempeh

Tempeh has been a favorite food and a staple source of protein in Indonesia for several hundred years, but was not widely available in the United States until the 1970's. Tempeh is a cultured food, like yogurt, made by the controlled fermentation of soybeans. Tempeh has a firm texture and a nutty "mushroom" aroma and flavor. It can be used as a main dish, and is delicious in sandwiches, spreads, soups and salads.

In Indonesia, you can buy uncooked tempeh in banana-leaf wrapped packets, or buy grilled "satay on a stick" from a street vendor. In this country, uncooked tempeh is sold at natural food stores and some supermarkets in 6 or 8 ounce packages, usually frozen. It is sometimes available as precooked burgers or cutlets. Tempeh shops in America now produce thousands of pounds every day.

Nutritive values

A complete protein food that contains all the essential amino acids, tempeh has the same quality protein as meat or poultry. It contains *no cholesterol* and only a trace of sodium. It is a good source of iron, vitamin E and lecithin.

Tempeh is an excellent source of fiber, an aid to lowering serum cholesterol, especially when combined in recipes with grains and vegetables. Vitamin B12 is produced by bacteria found abundantly in nature on plant material. The amount of this vitamin in tempeh depends on the numbers of these bacteria that grow along with the tempeh culture. This can vary from batch to batch, so tempeh should not be relied upon as a good source of B12.

How tempeh is made

Partially cooked soybeans are mixed with a friendly culture, *rhizosporus oligosporus* (tempeh starter), then the beans are spread out in flat sheets, about a half-inch thick, and incubated at 88°F. for 28 to 32 hours. Tempeh can be made from a variety of other beans and legumes, and with blends of whole grains, like rice, barley and millet. The nutritional analysis of recipes in this book is based on tempeh made entirely from soybeans.

Directions for making tempeh at home are described in this book by Cynthia Bates, director of The Tempeh Lab, in Summertown, Tennessee. She pioneered commercial production of tempeh starter in this country and ships starter to tempeh growers all over the world.

Storing tempeh

Fresh or defrosted tempeh will keep 3 to 4 days in a refrigerator at 40°F. and at least 6 months or more in a freezer. When putting fresh tempeh into a refrigerator or freezer, don't stack the packages because heat from one package to another will encourage the culturing process to continue.

Cooking Tempeh

Tempeh is easy to use, but must be thoroughly cooked. If using tempeh without further cooking, as in spreads or salads, **tempeh must be steamed or simmered for 25 minutes to thoroughly cook the product.**
Precooking: Steam defrosted tempeh for 10-15 minutes or simmer in a broth for that length of time. (Cut time in half if using full power in a 700 watt microwave oven.) Precooking in a broth tends to keep it juicy and plump.
Pan fried: Cut thin slices of precooked tempeh, coat with seasoned flour and fry in a little oil to serve as a breakfast food or as burgers or cutlets. You may need to cool the simmered tempeh to obtain thin slices. You will note in pan frying that tempeh quickly absorbs the oil in the pan, but will brown without adding more oil.
Deep frying: For many this is a favorite way to cook tempeh. Use a wide, deep, heavy pan like a Dutch oven or a wok. Use a quart of corn or peanut oil, which have high smoking points, and use a deep-fat frying thermometer. Heat the oil to 365°, quickly brown tempeh cut into strips or cubes, remove tempeh to a paper towel to drain. When oil is cool, strain the oil into a clean quart jar, using a small piece of cheesecloth in a strainer. Cover and refrigerate the used oil. It will absorb some color and flavor from the foods fried in it, but can be used for pan frying and other cooking. If you re-use the oil for deep frying, add some fresh oil to the pan.
Other: Steamed or simmered in broth, then crumbled or grated on the large holes of a grater, tempeh can be used in many favorite and ethnic recipes.

Here's a global perspective on eating tempeh: Soybeans have been called "gold from the earth" and are the single most promising protein source for the future. Twenty times more protein can be produced from an acre of land planted in soybeans than from an acre used to graze cattle. Vegetarians make a personal statement about world hunger in their commitment to a soy-based diet. Tempeh is an economical, highly nutritious, easy-to-prepare food that non-vegetarians can enjoy.

Ingredients and Suggestions

Arrowroot: Used as a thickener, this powder made from the roots of the arrowroot plant and has more nutritive value than cornstarch. Dissolve in a little cold liquid before adding to sauces.

Coriander/Cilantro: The green, broad leaf herb known as cilantro in Mexico and Chinese parsley in the Orient is more pungent than parsley, and the little tan seeds of the plant make the aromatic dried spice known as coriander.

Garlic: Buy firm, fresh heads of garlic, buds should be pinkish in color. Store in a dry, cool place, not in the refrigerator. When sauteing onion and garlic for a recipe, I prefer to cook the onion a few minutes before adding the garlic so it retains more flavor.

Gingerroot: These tan, gnarled roots are sold in the produce section of supermarkets and are an essential ingredients of Chinese cuisine. Cut several "fingers" into inch-long pieces and keep in a plastic bag in the freezer. It will last for many months and a piece can be taken out as needed to peel, then chop or grate. Powdered ginger can be substituted, but the flavor is not the same as fresh, pungent ginger.

Grains and Pasta: *Brown Rice* is unpolished, adds protein, minerals, vitamins and fiber to your diet and cooks in about 40 minutes with 2 parts liquid to 1 part rice. A pinch of sea salt added to the cooking liquid will break down the cellulose and make it more digestible. Try other delicious grains such as bulghur, couscous and millet. The *rice noodles* that puff up when deep fried, used in oriental cuisine, are available at natural food stores. Chinese *fresh pasta noodles* (as in the Lo Mein recipe, pg. 51) may be found in supermarket produce sections. *Bean thread noodles* used in soup are in natural food stores, as are *soba or buckwheat noodles*.

Mirin: slightly sweet liquid made from cultured rice and spring water, this Japanese product adds flavor to marinades and sauces.

Nutritional Yeast: Use only *saccharomyces cerevisiae*. Grown on a molasses base, it's available in flakes or powder form, has a cheezy flavor and a yellow color from its riboflavin content. An excellent source of B vitamins (often fortified with B_{12}) as well as protein and essential amino acids. Use of this product should not exceed 1 Tbsp. of powder or 2 Tbsp. of flakes per person per day.

Oils: Use unsaturated, unrefined vegetable and seed oils, like *olive, corn, safflower, sunflower, canola (made from rapeseed), soybean or sesame. Dark sesame oil,* much used in oriental cooking, is thick, with a distinctive nutty flavor. It is not suitable for frying, but a little of it can be used to flavor a blander oil. Avoid *coconut and palm oil,* which are saturated fats that may lead to a build up of fatty deposits in your arteries. The best oils to use for deep fat frying are *corn* or *peanut* oil, because they have a high smoking point. Corn oil has lass saturated fat content when heated than peanut oil. If you are on a low fat diet or counting calories, instead of sautéing onions, garlic, peppers, etc. in oil, simmer them a few minutes in water or vegetable stock. Oils made from nuts (almond, walnut, etc.) are best used cold in dressings.

Shiitake mushrooms: Large dried mushroom form Japan, full of flavor. Soak in hot water to remove sand and grit, then slice and brown.

Soymilk: This has as much protein as cow's milk without the saturated fat or lactose content, and provides calcium in the diet as well.

Tamari: Our soy sauce of choice is a naturally aged *shoyu* made from fermenting soybeans and cracked wheat, with no coloring or preservatives added. It is available in a wheat-free variety for people with allergies. Read labels of commercial soy sauces sold under various brand names, many are made with corn syrup, caramel coloring and salt. Be careful of soy sauces labeled "light" in oriental stores, as they may nave a higher salt content. For a light, less salty soy sauce, dilute tamari with water. If on a low sodium diet, use tamari or soy sauce sparingly or substitute a little balsamic or rice vinegar for flavor.

Vegetable Stock: If you don't make your own stock, the granules or powders available in natural food stores make an excellent and convenient stock, using 1 teaspoon to a cup of hot water.

Vinegar: Apple cider vinegar is strong in flavor, Japanese rice vinegars are milder, especially white rice vinegar made from glutinous rice. Malt vinegar, a favorite in England, is medium in flavor, but more acidic than rice vinegar.

Making Tempeh at Home

by Cynthia Bates, director, The Tempeh Lab, Summertown, Tenn.

A temperature of 85°-92° must be maintained for 26-32 hours, so check possible incubation places with a room thermometer. Some people make tempeh in a warm attic, or a closet with a drop light. You can make an **incubator** from an oblong cooler that has long sides slanted toward the bottom, so a rack, cake or cookie pan can be wedged in, leaving air space above and below the pan. The culture needs oxygen to grow and space to discharge excess heat and humidity.

Cynthia Bates

Tape a **room thermometer** to the center of the inside lid. Place an **electric heating pad** (with its cloth cover) on the bottom of the cooler. Cut a small hole in the rim for the cord so the lid fits securely. Turn on the heat and check the temperature. After 12 to 15 hours, tempeh will produce its own heat, so check the temperature and adjust or turn off heat source.

Use **a 2 gallon pot** with cover. Wash and drain **2½ cups (1 pound) soybeans**. Add **8 cups water** to the beans, bring to a boil, cover and boil 20 minutes. Turn off heat and let stand for 2 hours. Pour off water and use your hands to split the beans. Squeeze them with a kneading motion, a handful at a time, for 3-4 minutes. Add water to beans and stir to cause hulls to float to the surface. Pour off hulls into a colander, put any split beans that come out back into pot. Repeat kneading, add water, remove hulls until beans are split.

To the **split beans** add **10 cups water** and cook for 1 hour at a bubbling boil, skimming off any hulls that float to the top. Don't worry if a few are left. While beans cook, prepare bags. Place **2 ziplock bags** (7" x 8") on top of each other on 4 layers of a thick clean towel. With a straightened safety pin punch holes through both bags every half inch in a grid pattern.

Drain beans, then knead in a towel until they are surface dry. Cool beans until cooler than skin temperature. Transfer to a large bowl and mix well with **2 Tbsp. vinegar**, using a metal mixing spoon, *not wood*. Add **1 tsp. tempeh starter**, mixing very well. Store unused tempeh starter in a waterproof container in the freezer.

Warm the incubator to 90°. Divide the beans between the two bags. Cover a cookie sheet or rack with 2 layers of **thick terry towel** and set the bags on them flat. Pat beans firmly into an even layer, making sure they fill the corners of the sealed bags. Set the pan into the incubator.

The first sign that tempeh is starting to grow is when the beans loose their shine and begin to look dull. At 12-15 hours, white fluff begins to show faintly. Tempeh will now give off heat, so check thermometer and adjust heat as needed. By 17-20 hours the white fluff will be longer and thicker, almost covering the beans. At 24 hours the beans will be almost invisible under the white mycelium (the fine threads that the starter produces). Gray or black spots will form around the pinholes, the natural result of sporulation, and indicate ripeness. If the temperature in the incubator gets too high, crack the lid. Between 26-30 hours the cake will be dense, tightly woven by threads of mycelium.

Tempeh gets most of its flavor in the last hours of incubation so be sure to let it grow long enough. Cut off a piece and see if the beans are solidly bound into a white cake marbled with gray or black. It will smell like mushrooms and may smell faintly of amonia; a thin slice will hold together without crumbling. Unfinished tempeh is crumbly and the beans a little crunchy.

Cool finished tempeh, wrap in plastic and refrigerate or freeze. Don't stack tempeh packages until well chilled or the culturing process will continue. Fresh tempeh may be steamed or simmered in a broth for 20 minutes, then cooled, wrapped and frozen.

Tempeh starter can be ordered from:

The Tempeh Lab
P.O. Box 208
Summertown, TN 38483

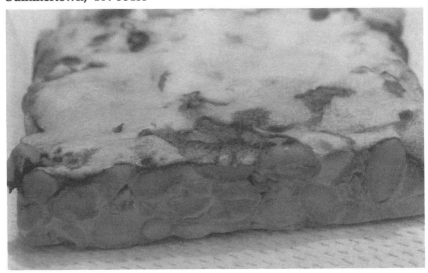

APPETIZERS

Croustades with Mushroom Filling

Yield: 32 croustades

Crisp, flavorful morsels to please a crowd.

Have ready:
> **1 loaf thinly sliced very fresh bread (32 slices)**
> **⅓ cup melted margarine**

Flatten each slice of bread with a rolling pin. Cut into rounds with a 2 ½" cookie cutter. Brush both sides of bread with margarine. Press into miniature muffin cups. Bake in a preheated oven at 400° about 10-12 minutes until edges are lightly browned. If made a day ahead, store in an airtight container.

For filling, dice into small pieces:
> **8 oz. steamed tempeh**

Sauté until lightly browned:
> **2 Tbsp. oil**
> **4 oz. mushrooms, rinsed, chopped**

Stir in and cook a few minutes:
> **2 Tbsp. flour** **dash of hot sauce or**
> **½ tsp. salt** **cayenne**
> **½ tsp. thyme**

When mixture bubbles, slowly stir in:
> **1¼ cups soymilk or milk**

Stir until thick and bubbly. Remove from heat, add tempeh and:
> **2 Tbsp. grated Parmesan cheese**

Fill tart cups, sprinkle tops with:
> **paprika**

Bake at 350° for 10 minutes. If filling is made ahead, cover and chill it; croustades may take a little longer time to bake with chilled filling. Whiz leftover bread into crumbs in blender and store for future use.

Per croustade: Calories: 109, Protein: 4 gm., Carbohydrates: 13 gm., Fat: 2 gm.

Dolmas (Stuffed Grape Leaves)

Yield: 20 rolls

Mint and cinnamon add zest to this classic Greek favorite.

Steam, cool and grate:
> **4 oz. tempeh**

Sauté until soft:
> **2 Tbsp. olive oil**
> **1 medium onion, chopped**
> **1 clove garlic, minced**

Combine grated tempeh and sautéed onion with:

1 cup cold cooked rice	**1 Tbsp. tamari**
¼ cup pine nuts, toasted in a dry pan.	**2 tsp. dried mint leaves**
2 Tbsp. minced parsley	**½ tsp. cinnamon**
2 Tbsp. currants	**½ tsp. oregano**

Rinse and drain:
> **1 lb. jar of grape leaves**

Put any torn pieces in the bottom of a wide kettle that has been lightly oiled. Place each leaf flat, shiny side down, removing stem. Press 1 Tbsp. filling into a round oblong and place in center of a stem end of leaf. Roll leaf up, folding in the sides. Pack rolls into kettle.

Mix and pour over the rolls:
> **¾ cup stock**
> **1 Tbsp. olive oil**
> **Juice of 1 lemon**

Place a heat-proof plate on top of the rolls and weight down with a heavy (2 lb.) can. Cover pan and simmer dolmas 45 minutes. Remove carefully from pan. Serve warm or cold.

Per dolma: Calories: 55, Protein: 2 gm., Carbohydrates: 4 gm., Fat: 2 gm.

Egg Rolls

Yield: 19-20 egg rolls

Everybody's favorite and fun to make. See photo opposite pg. 32.

Have ready:
>**1-16 oz. pkg. egg roll wrappers (19-20)**
>**8 oz. tempeh, steamed 15 minutes**

Grate tempeh and marinate with:
>**3 Tbsp. tamari**

Stir fry for 2 minutes:

2 garlic cloves, chopped	**2 cups Chinese cabbage,**
1 onion, chopped	**shredded**
1 green pepper, chopped	**2 Tbsp. oil**
½ cup celery, chopped	**2 tsp. gingerroot, minced**

Remove from heat.
Stir into vegetables:

4 green onions, chopped	**8 oz. can water chestnuts,**
with green part	**sliced in half**
1 large carrot, grated	**the marinated tempeh**
1 cup mung bean sprouts	

When filling is well mixed, pour into a colander to drain. It should be moist but not wet. Taste and add a little salt if desired.

Assembly: Keep wrappers covered with a damp cloth so they don't dry out. Make a paste with 1 Tbsp. flour and a few drops of water. Place one wrapper point side down in front of you. Put ⅓ cup of filling in oblong shape in center, fold up point nearest you, then fold in the sides. Moisten edges of remaining point with a dab of paste, roll over to seal the filling in, pressing edges gently to seal. Place rolls on a baking sheet. Continue until all rolls are filled. Bake or deep fry rolls at once so they don't get soggy. If fried only a minute on each side, rolls may be refrigerated or frozen for later use. When ready to serve, bake the pre-fried defrosted rolls at 350° for 10 minutes to reheat.

Deep-Frying: Heat 2 inches of oil to 365° in a wok or wide heavy pan that is at least 3 inches deep. Fry 3 at a time, about a minute or two on each side, turning, until golden brown. Drain on paper towels. If making a big batch, keep warm in a low oven. Serve with a dipping sauce.

Baked: Place rolls on lightly oiled cookie sheets, brushing tops lightly with oil so they do not dry out. Bake at 400° about 10 minutes, until lightly browned on top, turn rolls over, bake 5 to 10 minutes more.

Per serving: Calories: 118, Protein: 4 gm., Carbohydrates: 15 gm., Fat: 4 gm.

Dipping Sauces

Honey Mustard Sauce: Mix in a small bowl 2 Tbsp. Dijon style mustard, 2 Tbsp. honey and 1 Tbsp. rice vinegar.

Oriental Dipping Sauce: Mix in a small bowl ¼ cup tamari, 1 Tbsp. rice vinegar, 1 minced clove garlic.

Parsley Nut Balls

Yield: 48 balls

A holiday treat or a healthy snack.

Combine in a saucepan:

8 oz. tempeh, cut in half	**1 Tbsp. tamari**
1 cup vegetable stock	**1 bay leaf**

Cover, bring to a boil, then simmer for 25 minutes. Cool and drain tempeh, grate or process.

Bake at 350° for 10 minutes to lightly brown:
1 cup cashews or blanched almonds

Chop nuts coarsely, mix with grated tempeh and:
¼ cup mayonnaise or eggless salad dressing
¼ cup sour cream or yogurt
2 tsp. tamari

Have ready:
1 cup finely minced parsley

Press mixture into 1" balls and roll in parsley. Cover and chill.

Per ball: Calories: 37, Protein: 2 gm., Carbohydrates: 1 gm., Fat: 2 gm.

Tip

Almonds can be blanched in a microwave oven by arranging in a single layer in a flat dish; cover 1 cup nuts with ½ cup water and microwave on high for 2 minutes. Rub off skins.

Filo Triangles with Tempeh Filling

Yield: 48 triangles

Flaky, fluffy hot appetizers that melt in your mouth.

Have ready:
   ½ lb. filo dough, defrosted

Keep filo leaves covered with a damp towel so they don't dry out.

Steam for 10 minutes, cool and grate:
   8 oz. tempeh

Sauté until tender:
   2 Tbsp. oil
   1 medium onion, chopped small
   1 tsp. minced gingerroot

Add grated tempeh to skillet and sprinkle with:

2 Tbsp. tamari	**½ tsp. oregano**
½ tsp. garlic powder	**¼ tsp. allspice**

Stir together, then set aside to cool, adding:
   2 Tbsp. minced parsley

Have ready:
   ¼ cup melted margarine

Remove half the filo leaves and refreeze remaining leaves in the original package. Open up 1 sheet, laying it flat on your work surface. Brush sheet with melted margarine, fold in half and brush again. Cut into 2″ wide strips. Place a spoonful of filling at edge of one end of a strip, fold corner over into a triangle. Keep folding strip as a triangle. Brush top with margarine. Repeat process with other strips of remaining dough. These can be covered and refrigerated or frozen for later baking. Preheat oven to 400° and bake 15 to 20 minutes until golden brown. Serve hot.

Per triangle: Calories: 50, Protein: 1 gm., Carbohydrates: 2 gm., Fat: 2 gm.

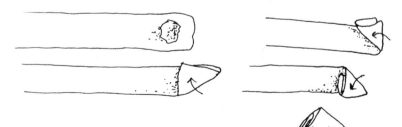

Pita Pizza Munchies

Healthy snack food for the whole family.

Yield: 48 triangles

Have ready:
6 pita breads	**1 green pepper, chopped**
6 oz. tempeh, steamed	**2 cloves garlic, chopped**
1 medium onion, chopped	

Sauté the onion, peppers and garlic in:
> **2 Tbsp. olive oil**

Grate the tempeh and add to pan when onions are soft. Sprinkle with:
> **1-2 tsp. pizza seasoning mix**
> **1 tsp. oregano**
> **1 Tbsp. tamari**

Cook a few minutes, stir in:
> **8 oz. tomato sauce**
> **⅓ cup sliced stuffed olives**

Set topping mixture aside. Cut each pita in half, then half again, making 4 pieces. Slit each crosswise; you will have 8 triangles from each pita. Place on cookie sheets and spread a spoonful of filling on top of each triangle.

Sprinkle with:
> **1 cup grated mozzarella cheese**

Bake at 375° about 12 minutes until cheese is melted. Serve hot. Filling can be made ahead and reheated before baking triangles.

Per triangle: Calories: 41, Protein: 2 gm., Carbohydrates: 4 gm., Fat: 1 gm.

Tip To mellow the flavor of strong onions, chop and soak in cold water for 20 minutes. Drain.

Parisienne Pate

Yield: 3 cups

A delectable dish for gourmet guests.

Simmer in a covered pan for 10 minutes:
> **8 oz. tempeh, cut in half**
> **1 cup vegetable stock**
> **1 bay leaf**

Remove bay leaf, add enough stock to make ¾ cup broth, pour liquid over:
> **2 cups sourdough bread, cut in small cubes**

Let bread soak. Cool and grate tempeh.
Sauté together until soft:
> **2 Tbsp. olive oil**
> **1 medium onion, chopped**

Combine in processor (or mash well):

the grated tempeh	**1 Tbsp. mirin**
the soaked bread	**½ tsp. marjoram**
the onion	**½ tsp. thyme**
2 Tbsp. tamari	**¼ tsp. nutmeg**

When mixture is smooth, pack into a lightly oiled 1 quart bowl. Heat oven to 350°. Cover bowl with foil and place in a pan of hot water. Bake 30 minutes; remove cover and bake 20-30 minutes more. Cool, unmold onto plate, serve with crackers or thin slices of toast.

Per ¼ cup serving: Calories: 127, Protein: 6 gm., Carbohydrates: 14 gm., Fat: 3 gm.

Tip

Spreadable Vegetables: Instead of serving crackers, spread sturdy slices of cucumber or zucchini, or stuff celery ribs.

Spread with Capers and Onions

Yield: about 2 cups

Combine in a saucepan:

    6 oz. tempeh   **1 bay leaf**

    ½ cup water   **1 Tbsp. tamari**

Cover, bring to a boil and simmer for 25 minutes. Cool and drain the tempeh and grate, or process.

Mix with:

    2 Tbsp. small capers,   **¼ cup mayonnaise or egg-**
        drained   **less salad dressing**
    2 green onions, chopped   **1 Tbsp. fresh lemon juice**
        fine
    ¼ cup celery, chopped very
        fine

Mixture should be of spreading consistency. Cover and chill.

Per ¼ cup serving: Calories: 93, Protein: 4 gm., Carbohydrates: 2 gm., Fat: 6 gm.

Green Onion and Parsley Spread

Yield: 1½ cups

Combine in a saucepan:

    4 oz. tempeh   **1 Tbsp. tamari**

    ½ cup water   **1 bay leaf**

Cover, bring to a boil and simmer for 25 minutes. Cool and drain the tempeh and grate, or process. Chop small:

    2 green onions, including green part

Combine grated tempeh, chopped onions and:

    2 Tbsp. parsley, minced
    2 Tbsp. mayonnaise or eggless salad dressing
    2 Tbsp. sour cream or yogurt

Per ¼ cup serving: Calories: 83, Protein: 4 gm., Carbohydrates: 2 gm., Fat: 5 gm.

Cashew Olive Spread

Yield: 1½ cups

Combine in a saucepan:

4 oz. tempeh	**1 Tbsp. tamari**
½ cup water	**1 bay leaf**

Cover, bring to a boil and simmer for 25 minutes. Cool and drain the tempeh and grate, or process.

Toast in a dry pan or bake at 350° for 10 minutes:
½ cup cashews

Chop cashews coarsely. Mix nuts and grated tempeh with:
⅓ cup sliced stuffed olives
2 Tbsp. sour cream or yogurt
2 Tbsp. mayonnaise or eggless salad dressing

If mixture is not moist and spreadable, add a little more salad dressing. Chill. Serve with crackers or thin slices of toasted sourdough bread.

Per ¼ cup serving: Calories: 159, Protein: 6 gm., Carbohydrates: 5 gm., Fat: 7 gm.

Ginger Tamari Tidbits

Yield: 40

Tangy bite-size morsels to serve hot or cold.

Steam for 10 minutes:
4 oz. tempeh

Chill tempeh while making marinade, so it will slice easily. Mix in a small bowl:

2 Tbsp. catsup	**1 tsp. dark sesame oil**
1 Tbsp. tamari	**1 inch gingerroot, chopped**
1 Tbsp. mirin	**fine or grated**
1 tsp. honey	**¼ tsp. garlic powder**

Cut the tempeh into 40 small pieces and mix with sauce gently so tempeh doesn't crumble. Cover and chill several hours or overnight. Place in a single layer in a baking pan, coating with the sauce, and bake at 350° for 2 minutes. Stick a toothpick in each piece to serve.

Per tidbit: Calories: 10, Protein: 1 gm., Carbohydrates: 1 gm., Fat: ½ gm.

SALADS

San Joaquin Salad

Yield: 6 servings

Red pepper flakes spark this flavorful salad.

Simmer in a covered pan for 20 minutes:
> **8 oz. tempeh**
> **1 cup vegetable stock**
> **1 tsp. tamari**

Cut tempeh into thin short strips, marinate in mixture of:
> **2 Tbsp. tamari**
> **2 Tbsp. mirin**

Bring to a boil:
> **2 cups stock**   **½ tsp. salt**
> **1 tsp. hot sauce**   **¼ tsp. red pepper flakes**

Stir in:
> **1 cup brown rice, rinsed**

Cover pan and cook 35-40 minutes until liquid is absorbed. Turn out onto a platter, fluff with a fork, cover and let cool.

Mix in a salad bowl:
> **juice of 1 lemon**   **1 green pepper, diced**
> **3 Tbsp. olive oil**   **2 medium tomatoes, seeded**
> **2 small garlic cloves,**   **and diced**
> **minced**   **1 cup green onions,**
> **chopped**

Mix the cooled rice with the vegetables. Fry the tempeh strips quickly in:
> **2 Tbsp. oil**

Add tempeh to salad, toss gently and serve at once.

Per serving: Calories: 266, Protein: 10 gm., Carbohydrates: 20 gm., Fat: 5 gm.

Tip To seed a tomato, cut it in half and hold over a sieve placed in a bowl. Squeeze out seeds. Use the strained juice.

Mock Tuna Salad

Yield: 6 servings

Fresh herbs are delightful in this, use if you have them. Makes a good sandwich filling. See photo on front cover.

Simmer in a covered pan for 25 minutes:
> **8 oz. tempeh**
> **1 cup vegetable stock**
> **1 bay leaf**

Cool tempeh and grate. Mix in a bowl:

1 cup celery, diced small	**½ tsp. basil**
2 Tbsp. green onions, diced small	**½ tsp. thyme**
	½ tsp. salt
2 Tbsp. parsley, minced	

Add tempeh to vegetables. Mix for dressing:
> **½ cup mayonnaise or eggless salad dressing**
> **juice of 1 lemon (about ¼ cup)**

Stir into salad. If desired, sprinkle with:
> **¼ cup roasted slivered almonds**

Serve on lettuce or in sandwiches.

Per serving: Calories: 214, Protein: 8 gm., Carbohydrates: 4 gm., Fat: 15 gm.

Tomato Stars

Yield: 4 servings

Cut 4 tomatoes in wedges, but not all the way through. Place each on a plate in a nest of Boston lettuce. In hollow of each, heap mock tuna salad.

Sprinkle over the tops:
> **¼ cup toasted slivered almonds or cashews**

Stuffed Avocado

Yield: 6 servings

Slice 3 small avocados in half and rub cut surfaces with a cut lemon. Place on lettuce, fill each shell with mock tuna. Garnish with strips of pimento.

Ming Dynasty Salad

Yield: 6 large servings

This is a complete meal for a luncheon party or an elegant first course for dinner.

Have ready:
    8 oz. tempeh, steamed 15 minutes, cooled

Heat oil for deep frying. Fry, in four batches:
    1 oz. rice noodles

Fry only a few noodles at a time, as these puff up very quickly. Have paper towels ready to drain them on. Cut tempeh into small cubes and deep fry them, drain.

Shake in a small jar for dressing:

¼ cup oil	**1 tsp. honey**
2 Tbsp. tamari	**1 tsp. grated gingerroot**
2 Tbsp. mirin	**¼ tsp. 5-spice powder***
1 Tbsp. dark sesame oil	**juice of ½ lemon**

Mix in a large bowl:
    6 cups shredded lettuce or salad greens
    1 cup celery, thinly sliced
    ½ cup green onions, sliced
    ½ cup roasted cashews, cut in half

Toss vegetables with the dressing, then add tempeh and rice noodles, mixing gently. Serve at once on luncheon plates.

Per serving: Calories: 363, Protein: 11 gm., Carbohydrates: 15 gm., Fat: 9 gm.

*5-Spice Powder can be obtained at oriental or health food stores or you can make your own.

5-Spice Powder

Measure into a small container and mix well:

1 tsp. ground fennel	**½ tsp. ground cloves**
1 tsp. cinnamon	**¼ tsp. Szechuan pepper or**
½ tsp. ground star anise	**cayenne**

Keep tightly covered.

Monterey Mousse

Yield: 6 servings

A cool treat for a warm summer day that can be made ahead.

Simmer in a covered pan for 25 minutes:
>**8 oz. tempeh, defrosted**
>**1 cup stock**
>**1 bay leaf**

Cool, pour remaining liquid into a 2-cup measure. Grate or crumble the tempeh and set aside. Add enough vegetable stock to liquid to make 2 cups.

Place liquid in a saucepan with:
>**2 Tbsp. catsup**

Tear into small pieces:
>**1 10″ bar kanten (¼ oz.)**

Soak kanten for 30 minutes in ½ cup cold water. Strain into a sieve, and rinse with cold water, pressing excess water out. Bring the 2 cups of stock to a boil, add the kanten and do not stir until it dissolves, about 3 minutes, then stir, cook for 8 minutes, remove from stove and let cool a few minutes.

Add to kanten:

the grated tempeh	**2 Tbsp. parsley, minced**
1 cup celery, chopped small	**½ cup stuffed olives, sliced**
¼ cup green onions, chopped	**2 Tbsp. sour cream or yogurt**

Mix well. Lightly oil a six-cup bundt pan or ring mold. Pour in salad. Refrigerate for 1 hour. To unmold: an hour before serving, set out mousse at room temperature, inverted onto a plate lined with lettuce leaves.

Per serving: Calories: 116, Protein: 8 gm., Carbohydrates: 5 gm., Fat: 3 gm.

Tip

Kanten (agar agar) is made from sea vegetables, harvested, boiled in spring water, then bleached and freeze-dried in the snow covered mountains of Japan. It is a healthy alternative to gelatin, which is made from animal collagen. Kanten flakes are also available and 1 Tbsp. of flakes will jell 1 cup liquid.

Pineapple Shells with Fruit Salad

An elegant and beautiful luncheon salad.

Yield: 6 servings

Bring to a boil, then reduce heat and simmer for 25 minutes:
> **8 oz. tempeh, cut in half**
> **½ cup water**
> **½ cup apple juice**

Cool. Cut tempeh into small cubes and toss with a marinade of:
> **¼ cup apple cider or juice**   **2 Tbsp. mirin**
> **2 Tbsp. tamari**   **½ tsp. grated fresh ginger**

Cover tempeh and chill for several hours or overnight.

Slice in half lengthwise, cutting down through the leaves to the stem:
> **1 ripe fresh pineapple**

With a sharp knife, cut around the shell, removing the flesh. Cut center core out of flesh as you cut pineapple into chunks. Cover and chill.

Dip into boiling water for 30 seconds, then peel:
> **2 fresh peaches or nectarines**

Mix pineapple and sliced peaches with:
> **1 cup fresh strawberries**
> **1 cup blueberries or seedless grapes**

Stir in the marinated tempeh and:
> **½ cup mayonnaise mixed with**
> **2 Tbsp. lemon juice**

Spoon mixture into pineapple shells. Garnish with:
> **fresh mint leaves**

Per serving: Calories: 340, Protein: 9 gm., Carbohydrates: 35 gm., Fat: 16 gm.

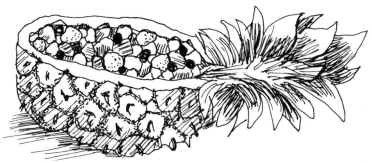

Bulghur Mint Salad

Yield: 6 servings

Combine tempeh with a grain for the nutritional punch of high quality protein.

Combine in a sauce pan:

8 oz. tempeh, cut in half   **1 cup vegetable stock**
1 bay leaf

Bring to a boil, reduce heat, simmer 25 minutes. Cool.

Combine in a bowl, stir and let stand 30 minutes:

1¾ cups boiling water   **1 cup bulghur**
1 tsp. vegie stock granules

Fluff with a fork. Cover and chill. Add:

the tempeh, drained and   **½ cup green onions,**
    grated or chopped   **chopped**
1 cucumber, diced   **¼ cup fresh mint, chopped**
1 tomato, seeded and diced   **2 Tbsp. parsley, chopped**

Mix in a small bowl:

⅓ cup olive oil   **1 tsp. honey**
3 Tbsp. lemon juice

Stir dressing into salad. Taste and add a little salt if desired. Serve on romaine or Bibb lettuce with a dollop of yogurt.

Per serving: Calories: 287, Protein: 11 gm., Carbohydrates: 25 gm., Fat: 6 gm.

Spinach Mushroom Salad

Yield: 6 servings

A classic salad, high in protein with the addition of tempeh. See photo on front cover.

Wash, tear up and dry:

1 lb. spinach, stems discarded
1 small head Boston lettuce

Steam for 20 minutes:

8 oz. tempeh

Dice tempeh in small pieces and fry in:

2 Tbsp. oil

Slice thinly, separate into rings:
1 small red onion

Rinse, wipe dry and slice thinly:
4 oz. mushrooms

Rub a salad bowl with a cut clove of garlic. Mix for a dressing:

juice of 1 lemon	**½ tsp. salt**
¼ cup light olive oil	**½ tsp. oregano**
2 tsp. honey	**¼ tsp. dry mustard**

Combine in salad bowl the spinach, onion, mushrooms and tempeh. Toss gently with dressing and serve at once.

Per serving: Calories: 221, Protein: 10 gm., Carbohydrates: 5 gm., Fat: 18 gm.

Warm Red Cabbage Slaw

Yield: 6 servings

Colorful and tangy.

Rinse, remove core and shred:
1 small head red cabbage

Let cabbage stand for 1 hour mixed with:
1 tsp. salt

Drain cabbage. Simmer for 20 minutes:

6 oz. tempeh, defrosted	**1 bay leaf**
1 cup water	**1 Tbsp. tamari**

Remove bay leaf, set tempeh aside to cool. Put cooking liquid in a small sauce pan. Add:
¼ cup cider vinegar
2 Tbsp. honey
1 Tbsp. arrowroot

Cook over low heat until sauce is thickened. Cook the cabbage in a small amount of boiling water until tender but crisp. Drain.

Cut tempeh into thin 2" strips and quickly brown in:
2 Tbsp. oil

In a large bowl, gently toss the cooked cabbage, the browned tempeh and the sauce. Serve warm.

Per serving: Calories: 127, Protein: 7 gm., Carbohydrates: 14 gm., Fat: 3 gm.

Hot German Potato Salad

Yield: 6 servings

Marvelous served warm, but good cold, too. See photo on front cover.

Cut in half, then simmer for 20 minutes:
> **8 oz. tempeh**
> **1 cup vegetable stock**

Cook in boiling water until tender:
> **6 medium large potatoes**

Drain potatoes. Sauté over medium heat (or cook in a microwave for 2 minutes) until soft:
> **2 Tbsp. oil**
> **1 large onion, chopped**

Stir into the onion:

1 Tbsp. arrowroot	**1 Tbsp. honey**
½ cup hot water	**1 tsp. salt**
¼ cup cider vinegar	**½ tsp. celery seed**

Cook, stirring, until sauce thickens and bubbles. Cut the drained tempeh into small dice and brown in a hot skillet with:
> **2 Tbsp. oil**

Slip skins from warm potatoes and slice into a bowl. Stir the sauce into the potatoes, add the tempeh and:
> **¼ cup minced parsley**

Serve warm.

Per serving: Calories: 322, Protein: 12 gm., Carbohydrates: 39 gm., Fat: 5 gm.

Bangkok Cold Noodle Salad

Yield: 6 servings

An Indonesian favorite that makes a complete luncheon.

Simmer for 25 minutes in a covered pan:
  8 oz. tempeh
  1 cup vegetable stock
  1 Tbsp. tamari

Drain, cut tempeh into small dice. Marinate tempeh in a mixture of:
  2 Tbsp. mirin   **1 Tbsp. dark sesame oil**
  2 Tbsp. tamari   **2 tsp. grated gingerroot**
  2 Tbsp. lemon juice

Cook for 2 minutes in boiling water:
  14 oz. pkg fresh Chinese noodles, cut in 3" lengths*

Drain, run cold water over noodles to cool, drain, cut into thirds.

Prepare vegetables:
  1 cup green onions, sliced ¼"
  1 medium carrot, grated
  1 cup celery, diced small

Roast for 10 minutes at 350°:
  ⅓ cup sesame seeds

Toss together vegetables, noodles, tempeh and dressing. Sprinkle with the toasted sesame seeds. Keep chilled if made ahead.

*If fresh noodles aren't available in your produce section, you can substitute ¾ lb. of linguine. Cook pasta 7-8 minutes until tender but firm, drain, rinse in cold water and drain again.

Per serving: Calories: 325, Protein: 15 gm., Carbohydrates: 42 gm., Fat: 5 gm.

Tip
Use a vegetable peeler to remove strings from ribs of celery before slicing celery.

SOUPS

Minestrone

Yield: 6 servings

A hearty meal-in-a-bowl soup and a great way to use up leftover pasta and other good things.

Cook in boiling, lightly salted water until tender:
> **1 cup elbow macaroni**

Have ready:
> **2 cups cooked pinto, red or kidney beans**
> **8 oz. tempeh, steamed 10 minutes, diced**
> **1-29 oz. can tomatoes**

Sauté until soft:
> **2 Tbsp. olive oil**
> **1 large onion, chopped**
> **2 cloves garlic, chopped**

Bring to a boil:
> **4 cups vegetable stock**

Add tomatoes and:
> **2 tsp. oregano**   **¼ tsp. cayenne**
> **1 tsp. basil**   **1 bay leaf**

Add sautéed onions and garlic, simmer covered 15 minutes. Add drained macaroni and beans. Simmer uncovered.

Heat a skillet, add:
> **2 Tbsp. olive oil**
> **tempeh, diced small or crumbled**

Sprinkle tempeh with:
> **2 Tbsp. tamari**

Stir fry a few minutes, then add to soup, and simmer about 5 minutes. Remove bay leaf. Serve in bowls with a sprinkle of parmesan cheese if desired.

Per serving: Calories: 309, Protein: 15 gm., Carbohydrates: 32 gm., Fat: 5 gm.

Red Lentil Soup

Yield: 8 servings

Red lentils are called "masoor" in India and are a treat anywhere. See photo opposite pg. 33.

Bring to a boil and cook 30 minutes in a covered pan:
2 cups red lentils, rinsed
9 cups water
a bouquet garni*

Steam for 10 minutes:
8 oz. tempeh

Sauté together until onions are soft:
2 Tbsp. olive oil
2 cloves garlic, minced
1 cup onions, chopped

1 cup carrots, chopped
1 cup celery, chopped

Add the vegetables to the lentils. Cook 15 minutes more, until lentils and carrots are tender.

Grate or cut small the tempeh and sprinkle with:
2 Tbsp. tamari

Pan fry a few minutes in:
2 Tbsp. olive oil

Remove the bouquet garni from lentils, add the tempeh. Add:
dash of cayenne

Taste and add a little salt if desired before serving. Serve with garlic toast.

Per serving: Calories: 291, Protein: 18 gm., Carbohydrates: 34 gm., Fat: 4 gm.

Garlic Toast: Slice a long loaf of Italian or French bread in inch thick slices. Mix ½ stick margarine with 4 cloves of mashed garlic. Spread bread, place slices on cookie sheet, bake in very hot oven 5 minutes then under broiler to brown.

Tip

Bouquet Garni: Cut a 5 inch square of cheesecloth or thin cotton. Place in it: 1 bay leaf, 2 whole cloves, 1 or 2 whole allspice or peppercorns, ½ tsp. thyme, ½ tsp. marjoram. Gather corners of cloth together and tie up with thin string or strong thread.

Vegetable Soup Provençale

Yield: 6 servings

A nourishing soup that may simmer at the back of the stove all day in a French farm house.

Have ready:

3 potatoes, peeled and diced

2 large onions, chopped

2 large carrots, sliced

2 ribs celery, sliced thinly

½ head cabbage, shredded

Put potatoes and carrots into a pan with:

2 cups boiling water

Cook covered for 15 minutes.

Heat in a large kettle and add:

2 Tbsp. olive oil

When oil is hot, sauté the onion a few minutes, add the cabbage and celery and sauté over medium heat 10 minutes. Add the potatoes and carrots with their cooking water.

Add to kettle:

4 cups vegetable stock

1-16 oz. can tomatoes, chopped

1 tsp. garlic powder

½ tsp. thyme

½ tsp. oregano

Bring soup to a boil, then add:

8 oz. tempeh, cut in small cubes

Cover pan, turn heat to low and simmer soup for 20-25 minutes. Taste soup and add a little salt if desired.

Just before serving, add:

¼ cup chopped parsley

Per serving: Calories: 221, Protein: 11 gm., Carbohydrates: 25 gm., Fat: 4 gm.

Bread soup: Place a thick slice of day old bread, lightly spread with olive oil, in bottom of each soup bowl. Ladle soup on top of bread. Sprinkle with parmesan cheese.

Egg Rolls, pg. 14

Indonesian Cauliflower and Noodle Soup

Yield: 8 servings

Cumin and coriander enhance the flavor of this savory dish.

Simmer for 15 minutes:
> **8 oz. tempeh, cut in small cubes**
> **1 cup water**

Cut into 1" florets:
> **1 lb. cauliflower**

Mix in a small bowl:
> **2 tsp. cumin** **¼ tsp. cayenne**
> **1 tsp. ground coriander** **1 tsp. salt**

Heat a skillet, add:
> **1 Tbsp. oil**

Sauté for 2 minutes:
> **1 small onion, chopped**
> **2 cloves garlic, chopped**

Add the mixed spices, the cauliflower and:
> **1 quart vegetable stock**

Cover and simmer soup for 15 minutes. Add:
> **4 oz. fresh Chinese noodles or soba (thin Japanese buckwheat noodles)**

Cook until noodles are tender, 6 to 8 minutes, adding the tempeh with its cooking liquid after 5 minutes.

Transfer to a tureen and sprinkle with:
> **2 Tbsp. minced fresh cilantro (Chinese parsley)**

Per serving: Calories: 150, Protein: 10 gm., Carbohydrates: 16 gm., Fat: 5 gm.

Tip Save out enough soup to heat and pack in a thermos for a hot lunch box treat.

Red Lentil Soup, pg. 31

Tuscany Two Bean Soup

Yield: 6 servings

Adapted from an old Italian recipe to include tempeh.

Wash and drain beans and soak overnight:
> **1 cup pinto beans**
> **1 cup navy beans**   **8 cups water**

Rinse beans, cover with 2 quarts water and add:
> **1 bay leaf**

Cook beans for 1½ hours until almost tender. Add:
> **2 carrots, diced**   **1 tsp. garlic powder**
> **2 ribs celery, diced**   **½ tsp. thyme**
> **1 large onion, chopped**   **½ tsp. marjoram**
> **1 tsp. salt**

Cook 30 minutes more. If soup is too thick, add vegetable stock to thin to desired consistency.

Cook for 15 minutes:
> **8 oz. tempeh, cut in half**
> **½ cup boiling water**

Cool tempeh and grate or dice small. Mix with tempeh:
> **1 Tbsp. tamari**   **½ tsp. sage**
> **½ tsp. thyme**   **½ tsp. marjoram**

Heat a skillet and add:
> **2 Tbsp. olive oil**

Cook the tempeh and spices about 10 minutes until lightly browned. Add to soup kettle. Mix well and ladle into bowls.

Per serving: Calories: 290, Protein: 18 gm., Carbohydrates: 34 gm., Fat: 5 gm.

White Bean and Potato Chowder

Yield: 8 servings

A vegetarian version of a traditional New England recipe.

Soak for 2 hours overnight in water to cover:
> **2 cups dried white lima beans, rinsed**

Drain, add 2 quarts fresh water, cover, bring to a boil, reduce heat and simmer 1 hour.

Add to beans:

4 large potatoes, in 1" cubes   **½ tsp. salt**
1 large onion, chopped

If not covered with 2 inches of water, add more water. Simmer soup 30 minutes until beans and potatoes are tender.

Remove 2 cups of beans and potatoes with a little of the liquid to a blender. Puree, then pour back into kettle, adding:

2 Tbsp. light olive oil

Taste and add salt and pepper if desired. Stir as puree thickens soup.

Ladle into bowls and top with:

¼ cup chopped parsley or chives

Per serving: Calories: 191, Protein: 9 gm., Carbohydrates: 31 gm., Fat: 1 gm.

Leek and Potato Soup with Watercress

Yield: 8 servings

Creamy and delicious as a first course or great for lunch.

Have ready:

2 lb. potatoes (4-5), peeled, diced   **8 oz. tempeh,**
1 lb. leeks, washed, thinly sliced   **steamed 10 minutes**
¼ lb. watercress, chopped   **3 Tbsp. minced parsley**
                                  or chives

Heat to boiling:

2 qts. water

Add potatoes and leeks to water, with:

1 tsp. salt

Cover pan and simmer about 30 minutes, until tender. Remove 2 cups of vegetables with a slotted spoon and mash. Return to pan with the watercress, and add:

½ cup soymilk
2 Tbsp. margarine

Cut tempeh into small cubes and deep fry, or pan fry over medium high heat in:

2 Tbsp. oil

Add parsley or chives to the soup, ladle it into bowls and float the browned tempeh cubes on top.

Per serving: Calories: 171, Protein: 8 gm., Carbohydrates: 14 gm., Fat: 5 gm.

Split Pea Soup with Barley and Tempeh

Yield: 8 servings

Serve with herb croutons for a satisfying Scottish meal.

Combine in a soup kettle or crock pot:

16 oz. green or yellow split peas, rinsed
10 cups water
⅓ cup pearl barley

2 carrots, diced
2 bay leaves
1 large onion, chopped

Cover pan, bring to boil, then reduce heat and simmer 40-45 minutes until peas are tender.

Steam for 15 minutes:
8 oz. tempeh

Dice tempeh into small cubes. Sprinkle it with:
2 Tbsp. tamari
1 tsp. garlic powder

Heat a skillet and add:
2 Tbsp. oil

Sauté the diced tempeh until it is brown. Add to soup pot with:
1 tsp. thyme

Simmer soup 5 minutes more, taste and add a little salt if desired.

Per serving: Calories: 246, Protein: 15 gm., Carbohydrates: 32 gm., Fat: 4 gm.

Herb Croutons

Remove the crusts from:
6 slices bread

Cut into 1″ cubes. Heat a skillet and add:
2 Tbsp. oil

Fry the cubes in the hot oil, adding:
½ tsp. thyme
½ tsp. oregano

When cubes are lightly browned, drain on paper towel.

SANDWICHES

Greek Pita Pockets

*Yield: 12 pockets - 6
servings*

A marvelous way to use the fresh herbs of summertime.

Have ready:
> **6 pita breads, cut in half to form 12 pockets
> 2 tomatoes, peeled, seeded and diced
> 2 cups iceburg or romaine lettuce, chopped
> 1 cup yogurt**

Steam 20 minutes and cool:
> **8 oz. tempeh**

Grate coarsely or crumble the tempeh. Stir in:

> **2 Tbsp. tamari   1 Tbsp. fresh basil,
> 1 Tbsp. lemon juice   chopped (or 1 tsp. dried)
> 1 Tbsp. fresh mint,   ¼ tsp. cinnamon
>   chopped (or 2 tsp. dried) ½ tsp. oregano**

Heat a skillet and sauté 1 minute:
> **2 Tbsp. oil
> tempeh mixture**

Add:
> **½ cup green onions, chopped**

Fry a few minutes. Warm the pitas if desired in a 350° oven for 5 minutes. Mix the tempeh with lettuce and tomatoes and pile into pita pockets. Top with yogurt and add bean sprouts if desired.

Per serving: Calories: 300, Protein: 16 gm., Carbohydrates: 32 gm., Fat: 9 gm.

Tip   To peel tomatoes, bring 2 cups of water to a boil in a small saucepan. Drop in a tomato and boil for 60 seconds. Remove with a slotted spoon, cool, cut out blossom end and slip off skin.

Tempeh Burgers

Yield: 6 burgers

Some day fast food chains will offer these sandwiches!

Steam for 15 minutes:
> **8 oz. tempeh**

Cool, cut crosswise into 2 thin slabs, cut each half into 3 pieces.

Have ready:
> **6 burger buns**
> **thinly sliced onion**
> **6 slices of tomato**

Heat a skillet and add:
> **2 Tbsp. oil**

Brown the tempeh slices in hot oil. Place a slice in each bun and top with tomato, onions, pickle. Add lettuce, mayonnaise or mustard if desired.

Per burger: Calories: 215, Protein: 10 gm., Carbohydrates: 19 gm., Fat: 9 gm.

Barbecued Tempeh in Buns

Yield: 6 servings

Juicy sandwiches to savor at a picnic or at home.

Cut in half lengthwise and simmer for 25 minutes:
> **8 oz. tempeh**
> **1 cup vegetable stock**

Cool, then cut into 6 pieces. In a small saucepan mix:

> **½ cup catsup**   **1 clove garlic, crushed in**
> **1 to 2 Tbsp. honey**   **press**
> **2 Tbsp. cider vinegar**   **¼ tsp. cayenne**
> **1 Tbsp. oil**

If you like a hotter taste, add a little hot sauce or more cayenne. Bring to a boil, reduce heat and simmer for 5 minutes.

Cover tempeh with barbecue sauce and serve in:
      6 whole wheat buns

Other cooking options are:
• Tempeh slices can be browned in 2 Tbsp. oil before covering with sauce if desired.
• Place tempeh in a single layer in a flat dish, cover with barbecue sauce, turn over and baste with sauce, then cover tightly with plastic and heat for 3 minutes in a microwave.
• Cover with foil and bake in a 375° oven for 15 minutes just before serving.
• Carry to a picnic and cook on a grill before placing in buns.

Per serving: Calories: 220, Protein: 10 gm., Carbohydrates: 26 gm., Fat: 7 gm.

Ruebens en Croissant

Yield: 6 servings

A French twist on an old favorite, but traditionalists can use rye bread.

Have ready:
      6 croissants, sliced in half
      16 oz. can sauerkraut, drained
      2 oz. Swiss cheese, sliced
      3 Tbsp. Thousand Island Dressing

Steam 20 minutes and cool:
      8 oz. tempeh

Cut in half crosswise, making 2 thin slabs. Cut each into 3 pieces.

Heat a skillet and add:
      2 Tbsp. oil

Brown the tempeh slices. Warm the sauerkraut. On each croissant half place a slice of tempeh, a spoonful of sauerkraut, a slice of cheese and a tablespoon of dressing. If desired, place under broiler a few minutes to melt the cheese before you add the dressing. Top with remaining half of croissant.

Per serving: Calories: 308, Protein: 13 gm., Carbohydrates: 18 gm., Fat: 18 gm.

Sandwich Loaf with Guacamole

Yield: 8 servings

An elegant luncheon dish that is made ahead.

Remove outer crusts from and cut lengthwise into four long pieces:
1 loaf unsliced whole wheat bread

Have ready:
1 recipe Mock Tuna Salad, pg. 22

Prepare the guacamole layer by mashing:
1 large ripe avocado

Stir into mashed avocado:

**2 green onions, finely
    chopped
2 Tbsp. fresh lemon or lime
    juice**

**¼ tsp. garlic powder
¼ tsp. hot sauce
1 pinch of salt**

Place the bottom slice of loaf on a platter. Spread with half the mock tuna salad. Place a slice of bread on top, spread with the guacamole. Place next slice of bread on top and spread with remaining salad. Finish with top slice of bread. Wrap loaf in waxed paper, then in a well wrung-out damp cloth and refrigerate several hours or overnight.

Before serving, "frost" the loaf with:
**1 cup cottage cheese, pureed in blender until smooth
or 8 oz. cream cheese, softened**

Decorate the top of loaf if desired with sliced stuffed olives or ripe olives. Use a very sharp knife to slice chilled loaf into 8 large slices. Serve on a plate with a fork.

Per serving: Calories: 340, Protein: 15 gm., Carbohydrates: 27 gm., Fat: 14 gm.

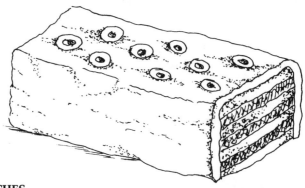

Super Hero

A spectacular sandwich to please a crowd.

Yield: 8 servings

Have ready:
> **1 long loaf sourdough or Italian bread**
> **3 large red peppers, marinated***
> **8 oz. tempeh, steamed for 15 minutes**
> **2 cups green leaf lettuce, rinsed**
> **1 large red onion, sliced thinly**
> **2 tomatoes, thinly sliced**
> **1 large avocado (optional)**
> **6 slices Monterey Jack cheese (optional)**

*Prepare marinated red peppers several hours or a day ahead. Preheat oven to 375°. Place peppers on baking sheet and bake 45 minutes until skin is blackened. Remove to a plate to cool and drain. Remove charred skin, stem and seeds.

Cut into thin strips and marinate in a mixture of:
> **⅓ cup olive oil**
> **½ tsp. oregano**
> **3 cloves garlic, finely chopped**

Cut the tempeh into half, crosswise, then each half into 4 thin strips.

Heat a skillet and add:
> **2 Tbsp. olive oil**

Quickly brown the tempeh strips, remove to paper towel Remove the red pepper strips from oil and spread the remaining garlic oil on the bottom side of the loaf half. Cover with a layer of the lettuce, then the red onions, the cheese slices, tomatoes, tempeh slices and red peppers. Top with a layer of sliced avocado, if desired, and the top half of the loaf. If you like, the top half of the loaf can be spread with mayonnaise or salad dressing. Cut carefully into 8 slices and serve on luncheon plates.

*Our thanks to Polly Pitchford and Delia Quigley, the authors of *Starting Over: Learning to Cook with Natural Foods*, whose marinated red pepper recipe is essential to this sandwich.

Per serving: Calories: 296, Protein: 10 gm., Carbohydrates: 29 gm., Fat: 5 gm.

Hummus and Tempeh Sandwich Spread

Yield: 3 cups

Simmer for 25 minutes in a small saucepan:
> **4 oz. tempeh**
> **1 bay leaf**
> **1 cup vegetable stock**

Cool tempeh while preparing hummus. Process until smooth or put through a food or grain mill (do not use a blender):
> **2 cups cooked chick peas (garbanzo beans)**

In a quart bowl, mix:
> **½ cup tahini**   **2 cloves garlic, put through**
> **½ tsp. salt**   **press**
> **juice of 1 lemon**

Whip with a fork until a smooth consistency is reached, adding a little bit of the chick pea cooking liquid. Stir in the cooked chick peas.

Grate the tempeh and add, with:
> **2 Tbsp. chopped green onions**
> **¼ cup minced parsley**

Taste and add a little more lemon juice or salt if needed. To use this spread as a dip for raw vegetables, thin it with more cooking liquid from the chick peas.

Per ¼ cup serving: Calories: 153, Protein: 8 gm., Carbohydrates: 12 gm., Fat: 14 gm.

Shiitake Mushrooms and Garlic Sauce

Yield: 6 servings

An easy recipe for learning to use these delicious Japanese mushrooms.

Steam for 10 minutes:
    8 oz. tempeh

Prepare marinade:
2 Tbsp. tamari	**1 Tbsp. arrowroot**
2 Tbsp. mirin	**½ tsp. honey**
2 Tbsp. lime juice	

Slice tempeh in half crosswise, then each half into 3 thin slices. Score lightly. Place in a dish and cover with marinade. Let soak, turning over once or twice.

Pour 1 cup boiling water over:
    ½ oz. dried shiitake mushrooms

Let soak for 20 minutes. Remove mushrooms, careful to leave any sand in the bottom of the dish. Pour off half a cup of liquid to reserve for sauce. Slice the mushrooms.

Prepare vegetables:
    3 cloves garlic, thinly sliced   4 green onions, in 1″ slices

Heat a skillet, adding:
    2 Tbsp. oil

Remove tempeh from marinade. Add mushroom liquid to leftover marinade for sauce. Fry tempeh over medium high heat until browned on both sides. Place on warm platter.

Add to hot pan:
    1 Tbsp. oil

Quickly fry the garlic, mushrooms and green onions, pour the sauce over them, cook 2 minutes, then pour sauce over tempeh and serve.

Per serving: Calories: 170, Protein: 8 gm., Carbohydrates: 10 gm., Fat: 11 gm.

Szechuan Tempeh with Almonds

Yield: 6 servings

The secret of stir-frying is having everything ready in advance, the vegetables, the sauce, the tempeh.

Steam for 10 minutes, cool and cut into thin 1" strips:
8 oz. tempeh

Prepare the vegetables:
1 cup leeks, green and white parts, sliced thinly
1 cup celery, sliced thinly on diagonal
1 green pepper, thinly sliced
1 large onion, thinly sliced in half moons
¼ lb. snow peas, ends trimmed
2 tsp. ginger, finely chopped

Pour boiling water over:
1 cup almonds

Slip skins off almonds, roast at 350° about 10 minutes.

Mix for the sauce:

1 cup vegetable stock	**1 Tbsp. arrowroot powder**
¼ cup tamari	**1 tsp. honey**
2 Tbsp. mirin	**½ tsp. 5-Spice Powder***

Heat a wok or large skillet over medium high heat. Add:
2 Tbsp. light sesame oil
1 tsp. dark sesame oil

Stir fry the tempeh quickly until browned, remove to paper towel.

Add to hot pan:
2 Tbsp. light sesame oil

Add onions, leeks, ginger, celery and green pepper. Stir fry a few minutes, add peas. Push vegetables to one side of pan, pour in the sauce, stir a few minutes until it thickens, then mix sauce with vegetables and stir in the tempeh. Serve at once on hot rice or Chinese noodles.

*See recipe on page 23.

Per serving: Calories: 389, Protein: 15 gm., Carbohydrates: 26 gm., Fat: 17 gm.

Sukiyaki with Broccoli & Cauliflower

Yield: 6 servings

A delightful Japanese medley of tempeh and vegetables.

Steam for 10 minutes:
> **8 oz. tempeh**

Cut into thin strips and marinate in a mixture of:
> **3 Tbsp. tamari**   **1 tsp. Worcestershire sauce**
> **2 Tbsp. mirin**   **1 tsp. honey**
> **1 Tbsp. arrowroot**

Stir occasionally so tempeh is coated.

Prepare vegetables:
> **1 Tbsp. gingerroot, finely minced**
> **1 green pepper, sliced thinly**
> **1 large onion, cut in thin wedges**
> **1 large carrot, cut in matchsticks**
> **1 cup celery, thinly sliced**
> **1 cup broccoli flowerets**
> **1 cup cauliflower, thinly sliced**

Bring to a boil in a sauce pan:
> **1 cup vegetable stock**

Add carrots, broccoli and cauliflower and boil for 1 minute only. Drain at once, reserving liquid for sauce. Drain tempeh and add any remaining marinade to the vegetable liquid.

Heat a wok or large skillet and add:
> **2 Tbsp. oil**

Fry the tempeh slices until browned, remove to bowl. Heat pan, add:
> **2 Tbsp. oil**

Stir fry the onions and peppers a few minutes, add the celery, cook 1 minute, then add the carrots, broccoli and cauliflower. Cook 2 minutes.

Pour the liquid into the pan, bring to a simmer, add the tempeh and:
> **2 Tbsp. tamari**

Serve with cooked brown rice. Sauce will be thin.

Per serving: Calories: 225, Protein: 10 gm., Carbohydrates: 17 gm., Fat: 13 gm.

Chinaman's Purse

Yield: 8 servings

Individual stir fries, baked in a large crusty pouch, a family favorite.

In a large bowl, combine:
> 1 Tbsp. dry yeast   ¼ cup warm water
> 1 tsp. honey

Let mixture sit for 5 minutes. Stir in:
> 1 cup warm water   4 cups flour (half whole
> 2 Tbsp. oil   wheat, half unbleached
> ½ tsp. salt   white)

Knead dough 5 to 10 minutes, until smooth and elastic. Put a little oil in a bowl, roll dough around to coat, then cover bowl with plastic wrap and put in warm place to rise until double in size.

Steam for 10 minutes:
> 8 oz. tempeh

Cool, cut in small dice or crumble. Stir into tempeh:
> 2 Tbsp. tamari   1" gingerroot, minced

Prepare vegetables for filling:
> 1 large onion, chopped   1 carrot, grated
> 1 green pepper, chopped   2 cups cabbage, shredded
> 1 cup celery, thinly sliced 2 cups mung bean sprouts,
>   rinsed

Heat a wok or large skillet and add:
> 2 Tbsp. light sesame oil
> 1 tsp. dark sesame oil

Add the tempeh to pan and brown over medium high heat. Remove to paper towel.

Heat pan, add:
> 2 Tbsp. oil

Stir fry onion and pepper 2-3 minutes, add cabbage and celery, fry 2 minutes more.

Stir in:
> the carrots   1 Tbsp. tamari
> the bean sprouts

Pour vegetables into a large bowl to cool. Punch down dough, divide into 8 smaller balls. Roll each ball out into a big circle about ¼″ thick. Mix tempeh with vegetables. Place a portion of filling in center of dough circle, leaving any excess liquid in bottom of bowl. Pull sides of dough up to cover filling and twist at the top to close. Place on lightly oiled baking sheet. Let rise 15 minutes. Preheat oven to 375°. Bake "purses" about 20 minutes until lightly browned. If made ahead, remove to a rack at once so bottoms don't get soggy and reheat in 350° oven for 10 minutes just before serving.

Per serving: Calories: 387, Protein: 15 gm., Carbohydrates: 50 gm., Fat: 14 gm.

Sweet and Sour Tempeh

Yield: 6 servings

This is a favorite of students in my cooking classes.

Cook for 10 minutes:
> **8 oz. tempeh, cut into thin 1″ squares**
> **1 cup vegetable stock**
> **1 Tbsp. tamari**

Drain tempeh, reserving liquid for sauce. Heat a skillet and sauté tempeh until lightly browned in:
> **2 Tbsp. oil**

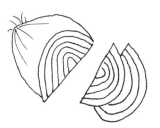

Drain, adding liquid to sauce:
> **1-15 oz. can pineapple tidbits**

Have ready:
> **1 green pepper, cut in 1″ squares**
> **1 onion, cut in thin half-moons**

Add peppers and onions to:
> **1 cup boiling water**

Bring to a boil again and drain. Put liquid from tempeh and pineapple juice into a measuring cup and add enough water to make 2 cups.

Stir in:
> **2 Tbsp. honey**   **2 Tbsp. arrowroot**
> **2 Tbsp. tamari**   **¼ cup cider vinegar**

Cook sauce until thickened and bubbly, then combine with peppers, onion, pineapple and tempeh. Serve over hot rice.

Per serving: Calories: 234, Protein: 9 gm., Carbohydrates: 31 gm., Fat: 8 gm.

Mandarin Tempeh on Rice Noodles

Yield: 6 servings

An elegant dish fit for an emperor. See photo on opposite page.

Steam for 10 minutes, cut in half lengthwise, then in thin strips 2 inches long:

      8 oz. tempeh

Mix for a marinade:

    2 Tbsp. mirin   **½ tsp. dark sesame oil**
    2 Tbsp. water   **½ tsp. honey**
    1 Tbsp. arrowroot

Coat tempeh slices with marinade, cover and set aside, stirring from time to time to coat evenly.

Prepare vegetables:

    2 cloves garlic, chopped
    1 onion, cut in thin half moons
    1 sweet red pepper, thinly sliced
    ½ cup celery, thinly sliced on diagonal
    4 oz. button mushrooms, quartered
    1 Tbsp. gingerroot, finely chopped

Mix and set aside for sauce:

    2 Tbsp. tamari   **1 tsp. dark sesame oil**
    2 Tbsp. mirin   **1 cup vegetable stock**
    1 Tbsp. arrowroot

Have ready:

    ½ cup roasted cashews, cut in half (opt.)
    ½ cup peas, fresh or frozen blanched in boiling water

Heat a quart of corn oil to 365° for deep frying. Fry, a few at a time as they puff up in a second:

    2 oz. rice noodles

Have paper towels ready to drain noodles on. Remove tempeh from marinade, drain it, add any leftover marinade to the sauce. Deep fry tempeh, about a third at a time, keeping pieces separate with a slotted spoon. When tempeh turns brown, lift out onto paper towels.

Heat a wok or large skillet. Add:

    2 Tbsp. light sesame oil
    1 tsp. dark sesame oil

Mandarin Tempeh

Over medium high heat, stir fry all the vegetables except green onions for 2 minutes; add green onions, cook 1 minute more. Add cashews. Push to one side of pan, add the sauce and cook until it thickens. Add the peas, then stir fried tempeh into the sauce. Pour onto platter or individual plates and surround with rice noodles.

Per serving: Calories: 310, Protein: 11 gm., Carbohydrates: 32 gm., Fat: 15 gm.

Cabbage Stir Fry with Ginger & Sesame

Yield: 6 servings

Economical and easy to make, with a lot of flavor.

Simmer in a covered sauce pan for 10 minutes:
>**8 oz. tempeh, cut in half**   **1 Tbsp. tamari**
>**1 cup vegetable stock**   **¼ tsp. garlic powder**

Drain, reserving liquid for sauce. Dice tempeh small.

Add to tempeh liquid:
>**½ cup vegetable stock**
>**2 Tbsp. tamari**   **1 Tbsp. arrowroot**

Roast in a dry skillet or in an oven at 350° until browned:
>**2 Tbsp. sesame seeds**

Have ready:
>**6 cups Chinese cabbage or Napa, shredded**
>**1 Tbsp. gingerroot, finely chopped**
>**1 cup chopped onion**

Heat a wok or large skillet and add:
>**2 Tbsp. light sesame oil**   **2 tsp. dark sesame oil**

When oil is hot, quickly brown the diced tempeh and remove. Add to pan:
>**1 Tbsp. light sesame oil**

Stir fry the onion and ginger 3 minutes, then add the cabbage and cook about 5 minutes. Pour in the liquid, bring to a simmer, stir in the tempeh and the sesame seeds. Serve at once with brown rice.

Per serving: Calories: 208, Protein: 11 gm., Carbohydrates: 10 gm., Fat: 12 gm.

Pizza, pg. 54
Calzone, pg. 55

Far East Fried Rice with Sunflower Seeds

Yield: 8 servings

A nutritionally complete meal, colorful and satisfying.

Cook until liquid is absorbed and rice is tender:
> **2 cups brown rice**
> **4 cups water**
> **½ tsp. salt**

Steam for 10 minutes:
> **8 oz. tempeh**

Mix in a small bowl for a marinade:
> **¼ cup tamari**
> **1″ gingerroot, minced**
> **2 cloves garlic, minced**

Dice tempeh small, let stand in marinade 30 minutes.

Toast in a dry skillet until lightly browned:
> **½ cup sunflower seeds**

Have ready:
> **2 onions, cut into thin half moons**
> **2 small zucchini, thinly sliced**
> **1 green or red pepper, in half-inch pieces**

Crumble the dry rice into a large bowl so grains separate. Lift tempeh from marinade with slotted spoon onto a plate. Save marinade to add to rice.

Heat a wok or large skillet and add:
> **2 Tbsp. oil**
> **1 tsp. dark sesame oil**

When oil is hot, add tempeh and quickly brown it. Remove to platter. Add to pan:
> **1 Tbsp. oil**

Over medium high heat, quickly stir fry the onions and peppers. Add zucchini and cook 1 minute more. Stir in the rice and cook, stirring, until rice is heated through. Stir in reserved marinade. Add a little more tamari if desired. Stir in browned tempeh and sunflower seeds.

Heap mixture onto serving platter and top with:
2 green onions, sliced ¼" thick

Per serving: Calories: 365, Protein: 15 gm., Carbohydrates: 38 gm., Fat: 12 gm.

Lo Mein with Fresh Chinese Noodles
Yield: 8 servings

This makes a large amount but is very good cold for lunch the next day.

Simmer for 10 minutes:
8 oz. tempeh   **2 Tbsp. tamari**
½ cup water

Drain tempeh and dice small.

Have ready:
4 green onions, cut ¼"   **1 large onion, cut in thin**
slices   **half moons**
4 oz. mushrooms, sliced   **1 red bell pepper, diced**
2 cups bok choy or Chinese   **1 green pepper, diced**
cabbage, chopped   **1-8 oz. can water chestnuts,**
1 cup celery, diced   **sliced**

Mix for sauce and set aside:
1 cup vegetable stock   **1 Tbsp. arrowroot**
2 Tbsp. tamari   **½ tsp. 5-Spice Powder (pg. 23)**

Heat a large kettle of boiling, salted water and add:
1-14 oz. pkg. of fresh Chinese noodles

Cook only 2 minutes, noodles should be tender but firm. Drain, set aside but keep warm.

Heat a wok or large skillet, add:
2 Tbsp. light sesame oil

Quickly stir fry the tempeh, remove to warm dish. Add to pan:
2 Tbsp. oil

Stir fry onion and pepper 2 minutes, add cabbage, mushrooms and green onions, cook a few minutes, add water chestnuts. Push vegetables to one side, add sauce, cook until it thickens, stir in the browned tempeh cubes. Toss with the cooked noodles to mix well.

Per serving: Calories: 369, Protein: 15 gm., Carbohydrates: 46 gm., Fat: 13 gm.

ITALIAN

Lasagne with Tofu and Tempeh

Yield: 8 servings

Have ready:
> **8 oz. tempeh, steamed 10 minutes**
> **1-32 oz. jar Italian style tomato sauce**

Grate the tempeh and add to the sauce.

For the ricotta-like tofu layer, drain, place on a clean towel and weight down:
> **1½ to 2 lbs. tofu**

When tofu is quite firm, combine it in a processor (or mash in a bowl) with:

¼ cup oil	**1 tsp. oregano**
¼ cup fresh lemon juice	**2 Tbsp. fresh minced basil**
1 tsp. salt	**(or 2 tsp. dried)**

Cook in boiling water until tender but firm:
> **½ lb. lasagne noodles (9 large)**

Lightly oil a 9″ X 13″ casserole. Cover the bottom of the dish with a third of the sauce. Place a layer of noodles, spread with half the tofu mixture, half the remaining sauce. Add a layer of noodles, remaining tofu, then another layer of noodles and spread rest of sauce over them. If desired, top with 1 cup grated mozzarella cheese or Nutritional Yeast Sauce (pg. 63). Preheat oven to 350°, cover pan with foil and bake 20 minutes, uncover pan and bake 20 minutes more.

Per serving: Calories: 346, Protein: 19 gm., Carbohydrates: 34 gm., Fat: 10 gm.

Potato Tomato Scallop with Shiitake Mushrooms

Yield: 6 servings

Traditionally made with mussels in Italy, tempeh and mushrooms make a great vegetarian version.

Steam until tender but firm:
5 medium potatoes

Steam for 10 minutes and cool:
8 oz. tempeh

Place in a small bowl:
5 large shiitake mushrooms

Pour over mushrooms and let soak 30 minutes:
1 cup boiling water

Grate tempeh and mix in a bowl with:

½ cup toasted bread crumbs	**1 Tbsp. tamari**
¼ cup parsley, minced	**1 tsp. oregano**
2 cloves garlic, chopped	**1 tsp. thyme**

Oil the bottom of a wide 2-qt. baking dish with:
1 Tbsp. olive oil

Slip skins from steamed potatoes and slice into the baking dish, over lapping slightly. Sprinkle potatoes with:
1 Tbsp. olive oil

Remove mushrooms from soaking water and slice thinly. Add mushrooms to tempeh mixture. Spread this mixture on top of the potatoes. Slice and lay on top:
2 large fresh tomatoes

If tomatoes are not in season, use canned tomatoes cut in half or sun dried tomatoes that have been soaked in hot water. Sprinkle with:
2 Tbsp. fresh basil, chopped (or 1 tsp. dried)

You can also sprinkle the top with a little parmesan cheese, if desired. Bake the dish at 350° for 30 minutes.

Per serving: Calories: 229, Protein: 11 gm., Carbohydrates: 26 gm., Fat: 5 gm.

Pizza with Sun-Dried Tomatoes

Yield: 2-12" pizzas or 1 large cookie sheet

See photo opposite pg. 49.

For crust, combine in a mixing bowl:
> **1 Tbsp. yeast**
> **¼ cup warm water**
> **1 tsp. honey**

Let stand for 5 minutes, then mix in:

1 cup warm water	**½ tsp. each oregano and**
2 Tbsp. olive oil	**basil**
½ tsp. salt	**4 cups flour**

Add a little more flour if needed to make a workable dough. Knead for 10 minutes until smooth and elastic. Oil a clean bowl and turn dough around to coat. Cover bowl and set in a warm place to rise until double, about 1 hour.

For filling, pour:
> **½ cup boiling water**

Over:
> **½ cup sun dried tomatoes***

Let stand while preparing tempeh. Steam for 10 minutes:
> **8 oz. tempeh**

Cool and grate or crumble tempeh. Mix tempeh with:
> **2 Tbsp. tamari**
> **1 tsp. oregano**
> **¼ tsp. chili pepper flakes**

Heat a large skillet, add:
> **2 Tbsp. olive oil**

Fry the tempeh until lightly browned. Punch down dough and roll out to fit a lightly oiled pan (if a 15-inch round pan is used it will be a deep-pan pizza). Let dough rise about 10 minutes. Put tempeh on.

Slice thinly:
> **1 large onion**
> **1 green pepper**
> **1 cup mushrooms**

Drain tomatoes and arrange on dough with onions, peppers and mushrooms. Add sliced olives and grated cheese if desired. Dough will continue to rise as you are preparing toppings. Preheat oven to 400°. Bake pizza 20-25 minutes. Cut circles into 4 wedges each, or cut rectangle into 8 large pieces.

*If you can't obtain sundried tomatoes, substitute a 8 oz. can of tomato sauce and spread on pizza before adding toppings.

Per serving: Calories: 338, Protein: 15 gm., Carbohydrates: 49 gm., Fat: 4 gm.

Calzone

Yield: 9 large

Delicious hot and a lunch box treat when cold. See photo opposite pg. 49.

Use the dough directions as for pizza. While dough is rising, make filling. Sauté together until onions are soft:

2 Tbsp. olive oil
1 large onion, chopped
1 green pepper, chopped

Add:

**8 oz. tempeh, steamed 10
    minutes, cooled, grated**
8 oz. can tomato sauce
2 Tbsp. tamari

1 tsp. oregano
1 tsp. basil
½ tsp. garlic powder
**¼ tsp. red pepper flakes
    (opt.)**

Punch dough down and divide into 9 balls. Roll each ball out to a circle ¼" thick. Place ¼ cup filling in center. If desired, a little grated cheese can be added. Fold dough over the filling into a half circle. Moisten edge with a dab of water to seal well. Flute the edges with tines of a fork. Prick the tops all over with a fork. Place calzone on lightly oiled cookie sheets. Preheat oven to 375° and bake 20-25 minutes until lightly browned. Remove to a rack to cool so bottoms don't get soggy. Serve warm or cold.

Per serving: Calories: 304, Protein: 13 gm., Carbohydrates: 44 gm., Fat: 4 gm.

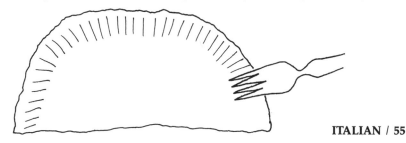

Tetrazinni Turino

Yield: 6 servings

A light northern Italian sauce with zesty flavor.

Steam for 10 minutes, cool and cut into small dice:
8 oz. tempeh

Sprinkle with:
2 Tbsp. tamari

Let tempeh stand while making sauce. Have ready:
1 cup onions, chopped
1 green pepper, chopped
4 oz. can pimentos, drained, chopped

In a large sauce pan, heat:
2 Tbsp. olive oil

Sauté the onions and pepper until soft. Stir in:
3 Tbsp. flour
½ tsp. salt
¼ tsp. cayenne

Cook a few minutes, stir in slowly:
1 cup soymilk
1 cup vegetable stock

Let stock simmer a few minutes. Heat a skillet, add:
2 Tbsp. oil

Stir fry the tempeh a few minutes, then add to sauce. Add the chopped pimentos.

Cook in boiling, salted water until tender but firm:
1 lb. linguine

Drain pasta. Toss pasta with tempeh sauce and:
2 Tbsp. parmesan cheese, grated

This can be made ahead and put into a lightly oiled casserole. Before serving, bake at 350° until bubbly.

Per serving: Calories: 420, Protein: 18 gm., Carbohydrates: 53 gm., Fat: 7 gm.

Mini Shells Italiano

Yield: 6 servings

Leftovers are good served as a cold pasta salad the next day.

Steam for 10 minutes, cool and grate:
8 oz. tempeh

Sauté until onions soften:
2 Tbsp. olive oil	**1 large onion, chopped**
3 cloves garlic	**1 green pepper, chopped**

Add grated tempeh and sprinkle with:
2 Tbsp. tamari	**1 tsp. basil**
1 tsp. oregano	**1 tsp. marjoram**

Stir spices into tempeh mixture and cook a few minutes to lightly brown tempeh. Chop:
1-15 oz. can tomatoes or 2 large fresh tomatoes

Stir into tomatoes, then add tomatoes to tempeh:
1 tsp. honey

Simmer sauce a few minutes. Prepare, according to package directions:
2 cups small pasta shells

Drain pasta and toss with sauce. Serve in a large bowl. If desired, sprinkle with:
2 Tbsp. parmesan cheese

If made ahead, pour into lightly oiled baking dish, cover, and bake at 350° for 30 minutes or until bubbly.

Per serving: Calories: 240, Protein: 12 gm., Carbohydrates: 26 gm., Fat: 5 gm.

Tip
If your kids don't like onions, try pureeing them so you get the flavor without any visible pieces.

Scallopine with Red and Green Peppers

Colorful and full of flavor

Yield: 6 servings

Steam for 15 minutes:
   8 oz. tempeh

Cool tempeh, cut into thin strips and marinate in a mixture of:
   2 Tbsp. tamari
   2 Tbsp. mirin
   ¼ cup vegetable stock

Cut into thin wedges:
   2 large onions

Remove seeds and cut into thin strips 2″ long:
   1 green pepper
   1 sweet red pepper

Drain tempeh, reserving any leftover marinade. Heat a large skillet, add:
   2 Tbsp. olive oil

Quickly brown the tempeh strips and transfer to a warm platter.

Add to skillet:
   2 Tbsp. olive oil

Add onions and peppers and stir fry 5 minutes over medium high heat until tender but firm. To any remaining marinade add:
   2 cups vegetable stock
   2 Tbsp. tamari
   2 Tbsp. arrowroot dissolved in ¼ cup water

Pour sauce mixture over onions and peppers and stir until it thickens. Mix in the cooked tempeh. Serve over buckwheat noodles or brown rice.

Per serving: Calories: 214, Protein: 9 gm., Carbohydrates: 16 gm., Fat: 6 gm.

Stuffed Jumbo Shells

Yield: 4 servings

Steam for 10 minutes, cool and grate:
> **6 oz. tempeh**

Mix tempeh with:
> **2 Tbsp. tamari**

Have ready:
> **1 large onion, chopped**   **2 cloves garlic, chopped**

Heat skillet and add:
> **2 Tbsp. olive oil**

Add tempeh and fry quickly until lightly browned. Remove to a bowl.

Add to pan:
> **1 Tbsp. olive oil**

Sauté onion and garlic until soft. Stir in:
> **8 oz. can tomato paste**   **1 can of water**

Bring to a boil, add:
> **1 tsp. vegetable stock granules**
> **1 tsp. oregano**
> **1 tsp. basil**

Simmer sauce over low heat 10 minutes, then add:
> **2 Tbsp. minced parsley**

Set sauce aside. Bring a large kettle of water to a boil, add a little salt and:
> **8 oz. jumbo shells (about 15)**

Cook shells until tender but firm, drain. Run cold water gently over shells to cool them, and drain. Remove 1 cup of sauce from pan. Stir tempeh into remaining sauce. Stuff shells with tempeh mixture, placing them into a lightly oiled casserole. Drizzle reserved cup of sauce over shells. If desired, top with:
> **2 Tbsp. grated parmesan cheese**

Preheat oven to 350° and bake shells 25-30 minutes.

Per serving: Calories: 430, Protein: 18 gm., Carbohydrates: 53 gm., Fat: 7 gm.

Pasutici (Italian Flat Bread)

Yield: 12 squares

An Italian flat bread that makes a great lunch dish with the addition of tempeh. Dough can be made in a processor.

Place in bowl of processor:

1 Tbsp. yeast	¼ cup olive oil
1 tsp. honey	2 cups flour
1 cup warm water	

Process, then blend in:
1 tsp. salt
1 cup flour

Add more flour if needed to make a soft dough. Remove to a flat surface, cover and let rise for 1 hour until doubled. Press into a rectangle about ½ inch thick on a lightly oiled baking sheet. Let rise again until almost double. Prick dough all over with the tines of a fork.

Spread with tempeh topping:

8 oz. steamed tempeh, cut in small cubes or grated	1 onion, chopped
	2 tsp. oregano
2 cloves garlic, chopped	

Heat a skillet, add:
2 Tbsp. olive oil

Stir fry the tempeh, garlic, onion and herb mixture a few minutes until onions are softened. Spread on dough. Bake at 375° for 25 minutes. Cut into 12 squares and serve warm.

Per serving: Calories: 204, Protein: 8 gm., Carbohydrates: 24 gm., Fat: 3 gm.

MEXICAN

Mexican Rice with Almonds

Yield: 8 servings

This zesty casserole is a holiday feast dish in Latin America.

Steam for 15 minutes, cool and dice small:
8 oz. tempeh

Place in 2-quart cooking pan:
1 cup rice   **2 cups vegetable stock**

Bring rice to a boil, reduce heat, cover pan and simmer 40 minutes, until rice is tender and liquid is absorbed.

Heat a skillet and add:
2 Tbsp. oil   **1 green pepper, chopped**
1 onion, chopped

Sauté onions and peppers until soft. Add:
2 tomatoes, diced small   **1 tsp. garlic powder**
2 tsp. chili powder   **½ tsp. salt**
1 tsp. cumin

Cook a few minutes, add cubes of tempeh.

Roast in a shallow pan at 350° for 10 minutes:
½ cup almonds, chopped

Stir sauce and almonds into rice. Serve at once, or pile into lightly oiled baking dish to reheat later. If desired, add ¼ cup raisins to rice. Serve with sliced avocado and a scoop of yogurt cheese*.

Per serving: Calories: 216, Protein: 9 gm., Carbohydrates: 20 gm., Fat: 8 gm.

Tip

To Make Yogurt Cheese: Line a strainer with cheesecloth, place over a deep bowl, pour a quart of yogurt into cloth and drain off liquid for several hours. Twist ends of cheesecloth together, drain 2 hours more. Chill the cheese in the cloth.

Baked Enchiladas with Beans and Tempeh

Yield: 8 servings

This takes time to make but the results are incredibly good.

Have ready:
> **8 oz. tempeh, steamed**
> **12 large whole wheat tortillas**
> **2-15 oz. cans pinto beans**

For enchilada sauce, sauté (or cook in microwave for 2 minutes):
> **3 Tbsp. oil**
> **2 onions, chopped**

When onions are soft, sprinkle with:
> **2 Tbsp. chili powder**   **¾ tsp. salt**
> **1 tsp. cumin**   **⅓ cup flour**

Cook a few minutes (or 1 minute in microwave) Add:
> **5 cups water**

Bring to a boil, then simmer over low heat for 20 minutes (10 minutes on medium in a microwave in a 2 quart container, stirring occasionally). Grate the tempeh and add to sauce. Drain the beans and add liquid to sauce. Pour 1 cup of sauce into bottom of a lightly oiled 9" X 13" baking pan. On a hot, dry griddle, cook each tortilla for a minute or two on each side. Place a spoonful of beans in each and roll up. Place seam side down in the sauce. When tortillas are filled, pour remaining sauce over contents of dish. Bake at 350° for 30 minutes. If desired, top casserole with 1 cup grated Jack cheese or a recipe of Nutritional Yeast Sauce.

Per serving: Calories: 319, Protein: 16 gm., Carbohydrates: 44 gm., Fat: 4 gm.

Nutritional Yeast Sauce

Yield: about 2½ cups

Nutritional yeast adds a cheezy flavor to this delicious sauce.

Over medium heat in a heavy-bottomed pan, cook for about 10 minutes until you can faintly smell it:
> **⅓ cup flour**

Stir in:
> **⅓ cup nutritional yeast***

Slowly add:

> ¼ **cup oil**
> **2 cups warm water**

Cook, stirring with a whisk, until mixture is thick and bubbly. Add:

> **1 Tbsp. tamari or salt to taste**

*Use only nutritional yeast, not brewer's yeast.

Per ¼ cup serving: Calories: 75, Protein: 1 gm., Carbohydrates: 5 gm., Fat: 6 gm.

Easy Enchilada Casserole with Corn Tortillas

Yield: 6 servings

Have ready:

> **12 corn tortillas**
> **8 oz. tempeh, steamed**
> **1 cup sour cream or yogurt (opt.)**
> **1 cup grated Jack cheese or 1 cup Nutritional Yeast Sauce, pg. 62**
> **3 cups enchilada sauce (pg. 62) or salsa**

In a skillet, fry 5 minutes:

> **2 Tbsp. olive oil**
> **1 large onion, chopped**

Grate the tempeh, add to the onions, sprinkle with:

> **3 Tbsp. tamari**
> **2 Tbsp. chili powder**
> **1 tsp. cumin**

Fry about 5 to 10 minutes, to brown tempeh. Lightly oil a 9″ X 13″ baking pan. Pour 1 cup of the sauce on the bottom. Arrange half the corn tortillas for the bottom layer, spread with half the sour cream. Spoon on half the tempeh mixture, then 1 cup of salsa. Place a layer of the remaining tortillas, spread with sour cream, top with tempeh and remaining sauce. Sprinkle cheese on top or pour on strips of Nutritional Yeast Sauce. Preheat oven to 350° and bake for 30 minutes. If casserole is made ahead, bake a little longer.

Per serving: Calories: 381, Protein: 17 gm., Carbohydrates: 44 gm., Fat: 12 gm.

Taco Shells with Mexican Filling

Yield: 10 shells

Shells and filling can be made ahead. See photo on opposite page.

Preheat oven to 350°. Have ready:
10-10″ whole wheat tortillas
10 soup or cereal bowls
8 oz. tempeh, steamed 10 minutes, cooled
lettuce, tomatoes, sour cream and salsa

Press each tortilla into a bowl, crimping edges in a few places to fit. If desired, brush edges lightly with oil. Tortillas must be soft and flexible: sprinkle with a few drops of water and wrap in a damp towel if they are too dry. Place bowls on cookie sheets and bake at 350° about 15 minutes until shells are lightly browned and crisp. When shells are cool, wrap carefully in plastic bags. These will keep a week and can be reheated for 5 minutes in a 350° oven before using.

To make the filling, sauté in a hot skillet:
2 Tbsp. oil   **1 green pepper, chopped**
1 large onion, chopped   **2 garlic cloves, chopped**

Remove vegetables from pan. Grate or crumble tempeh into a bowl and sprinkle with:
2 Tbsp. tamari   **1 tsp. cumin**
1 Tbsp. chili powder

Mix spices with tempeh.

Heat skillet, add:
2 Tbsp. oil

Sauté the spiced tempeh until lightly browned. Mix with the cooked vegetables. Add:
¼ cup chopped green chilies (a 4 oz. can) or stuffed olives

Place fresh or reheated shells on plates or platters and in the bottom of each put:
½ cup lettuce, shredded
½ tomato, chopped

Top with a big spoonful of filling. If desired, add a dollop of sour cream and sliced avocados. Serve with salsa, chopped onions, wedges of limes.

Per serving: Calories: 160, Protein: 7 gm., Carbohydrates: 14 gm., Fat: 4 gm.

Burritos with Tempeh Filling

Yield: 10 burritos

Have ready:
8 oz. tempeh, steamed 20 minutes, cooled
2 cups cooked pinto beans
10-10″ whole wheat tortillas

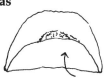

Grate the tempeh and mix with:
1 Tbsp. chili powder
½ tsp. garlic powder
½ tsp. cumin

Heat a skillet and add:
2 Tbsp. oil
1 onion, chopped

Sauté until the onion is soft, stir in tempeh and spices and cook 10 minutes more. Drain the beans and mash or process until smooth, adding a little bean liquid if too stiff. Stir the beans into the tempeh and onion mixture. Taste and add a little salt or dash of cayenne if desired. Keep filling warm. Heat a griddle or large skillet and fry each tortilla 1-2 minutes on each side, pressing down with spatula if they puff up. Keep tortillas warm with a towel. When all are cooked, place about ⅓ cup filling in center of tortilla. Sprinkle with chopped lettuce, chopped onion and a spoonful of salsa. Fold the bottom third over the filling, then fold in one side toward the center. Fold the other side in to overlap.

Per serving: Calories: 174, Protein: 9 gm., Carbohydrates: 21 gm., Fat: 5 gm.

Make Ahead Burritos to Freeze

Use same 10 whole wheat tortillas and filling. Make the filling but do not heat tortillas. Place ⅓ cup filling on each tortilla. Fold sides in, then fold up bottom and top like an envelope, moistening edges to seal. Wrap individually in plastic and freeze. These can be defrosted and heated through in a microwave, or thawed and baked in a conventional oven. To bake, place on a lightly oiled baking sheet, brush tops lightly with oil and bake at 350° about 20 minutes until lightly browned. Serve with side dishes of chopped onions, chopped lettuce and tomatoes, salsa, sour cream, guacamole or grated cheese. These are so handy to have on hand, we suggest you double the recipe and make a big batch.

Fajitas

Yield: 10 fajitas

Steam for 10 minutes:
8 oz. tempeh

Cool slightly, cut in long thin strips. Mix a marinade to pour over strips:
¼ cup tamari
2 garlic cloves, put through a press

Soak tempeh 30 minutes. Have ready:
10-10" whole wheat tortillas
1 green pepper, cut in long ½" strips
1 red pepper, cut in long ½" strips
10 green onions, trimmed to 6", cut in half lengthwise

Heat a griddle or heavy skillet to sizzling hot and quickly cook each tortilla, turning and pressing down with a spatula if they puff up. Cover with a towel to keep warm.

Heat a skillet and add:
2 Tbsp. olive oil

Fry the marinated tempeh over medium high heat until brown. Remove to paper towels. Heat in skillet:
1 Tbsp. oil

Cook the pepper strips a few minutes over medium high heat, then the onions. Arrange on each tortilla a few strips of tempeh, pepper and onion. Fold bottom of tortilla up, then fold two sides in. Serve with the tempeh and pepper strips showing.

Per fajita: Calories: 143, Protein: 7 gm., Carbohydrates: 14 gm., Fat: 3 gm.

Tostadas with Corn Tortillas

Yield: 6 servings

Set the toppings out so guests can build their own.

Have ready:

12 corn tortillas
1 recipe for Mexican Filling, pg. 64
3 cups romaine or iceberg lettuce, shredded

½ cup red onions, diced
½ cup ripe olives, sliced
2 avocados, sliced
2 large tomatoes, chopped

66 / MEXICAN

Heat the filling on top of stove or in microwave. Heat 2 inches of corn oil in a heavy skillet to 360°. Fry 1 tortilla at a time, about 30 seconds, lift out onto paper towels to drain. Put 2 tortillas on each plate and let guests add toppings. Other toppings might be salsa, hot sauce, sour cream or yogurt or grated Jack cheese.

Per serving: Calories: 382, Protein: 6 gm., Carbohydrates: 41 gm., Fat: 6 gm.

Chimichangas

Yield: 10

Crisp and golden, these Mexican favorites melt in your mouth

Have ready:
>**10-10″ whole wheat tortillas**
>**8 oz. tempeh, steamed for 20 minutes, cooled and grated**
>**1-4 oz. can green chilies, chopped**
>**oil for deep frying, (see pg. 9)**

In a skillet, over medium high heat, sauté for 2 minutes:
>**2 Tbsp. oil**
>**2 cloves garlic, chopped**
>**1 large onion, chopped**

Add the grated tempeh and:
>**1 tsp. cumin**
>**1 tsp. oregano**
>**½ tsp. salt**

Stir fry 2 minutes. Remove from heat, stir in chili peppers. Tortillas must be soft and pliable. If not, sprinkle them with a few drops of water and cook in a dry pan until softened or wrap in plastic and heat in microwave. Place about ⅓ cup filling near one edge of a tortilla. Roll up, tucking in the sides to seal in the filling. Fasten with a wooden toothpick. When all are made, heat at least 2 inches of oil in a wok or deep heavy skillet to 360°. Fry 2 or 3 rolls at a time for 1 to 2 minutes on each side, until golden. Lift out with a slotted spoon (do not use tongs) onto paper towels. Remove picks. Serve with salsa, guacamole and shredded lettuce on the side.

Per serving: Calories: 190, Protein: 6 gm., Carbohydrates: 13 gm., Fat: 12 gm.

Chorizo (Spanish Sausage)

Yield: 2 cups

A spicy treat that lends zest to casseroles or pizza.

Steam for 10 minutes and cool:
>   8 oz. tempeh

Grate the tempeh and add:
>   3 cloves garlic, put through
>   a press
>   1 Tbsp. chili powder
>   2 tsp. cider vinegar
>   1 tsp. cumin
>   1 tsp. salt

>   1 tsp. crushed red pepper
>   flakes
>   ½ tsp. thyme
>   ¼ tsp. coriander
>   ¼ tsp. cinnamon

Mix spices and tempeh well, cover and let stand overnight. Press into patties if desired, or fry in a little oil and toss with pasta. Good sprinkled on pizza before baking.

Per ¼ cup serving: Calories: 59, Protein: 6 gm., Carbohydrates: 2 gm., Fat: 3 gm.

Garbanzo Bean and Chorizo Casserole

Yield: 8 servings

Have ready:
>   1 recipe Chorizo

Soak overnight:
>   1 cup garbanzo beans, rinsed

Drain, add:
>   4 cups water

When beans are almost tender (1½ hours), add:
>   1 tsp. salt (opt.)

Sauté together:
>   2 Tbsp. olive oil
>   2 cloves garlic, chopped

>   1 cup onion, chopped
>   1 green pepper, chopped

When onions are soft, add the chorizo and cook for 5 minutes more.

Remove from heat, stir in:
½ cup ripe olives, sliced

Drain the beans, mix with the chorizo and:
1-8 oz. can tomato sauce

Pile into a bean pot or large casserole and bake at 350° for 30 minutes.

Per serving: Calories: 192, Protein: 10 gm., Carbohydrates: 17 gm., Fat: 4 gm.

Green Chili Sauce with Tempeh

Yield: 6 servings
A South of the Border dish for Tex-Mex food lovers.

Steam for 10 minutes, cut crosswise in half, then in thirds for 6 thin slices:
8 oz. tempeh

Make shallow diagonal cuts across tempeh and sprinkle with:
2 Tbsp. tamari

Let tempeh marinate while preparing sauce.

Sauté together until onions are soft:
1 Tbsp. olive oil
½ cup onions, chopped

Add to onions:
1-4 oz. can green chilies, chopped

Heat chilies, then stir in:
½ cup sour cream, at room temperature

Set sauce aside and fry tempeh slices in:
2 Tbsp. olive oil

Place tempeh on platter, pour sauce over tempeh, serve with cooked rice.

Per serving: Calories: 182, Protein: 8 gm., Carbohydrates: 4 gm., Fat: 8 gm.

Picadillo with Masa Harina

Yield: 8 servings

*A delicious recipe using masa harina, the flour used to make corn tortillas -
available in the Mexican food section of many supermarkets.*

Bring to a boil in a large kettle:
6 cups water

Stir in slowly, mixing with a big whisk:
1 tsp. salt   **2 cups masa harina**

Simmer mush 15 minutes over low heat, stirring frequently. Or cover
pan and microwave on high for 5 minutes.

To prepare filling, sauté until soft:
2 Tbsp. olive oil   **2 green peppers, chopped**
1 cup onions, chopped

Grate or crumble into the pan:
8 oz. tempeh, steamed

Sprinkle with:
2 Tbsp. chili powder   **½ tsp. salt**
2 tsp. cumin

Cook tempeh a few minutes, add:
1-4 oz. can green chilies, drained and chopped
1-15 oz. can tomatoes, chopped
½ cup raisins
⅓ cup stuffed olives, sliced

Lightly oil a large baking pan and line the bottom and sides with the
cooked masa harina, reserving a third for top. Pour in tempeh filling.
Top with remaining masa. Bake at 350° for 30 minutes.

Per serving: Calories: 256, Protein: 10 gm., Carbohydrates: 37 gm., Fat: 5 gm.

Posole

Yield: 8 servings

Omit raisins from Picadillo recipe and add to tempeh sauce:
2 cups hominy or whole kernel corn

Per serving: Calories: 264, Protein: 11 gm., Carbohydrates: 37 gm., Fat: 5 gm.

AMERICAN

Hawaiian Kebabs with Pineapple and Peppers

Yield: 18 kebabs

Exotic looking and wonderful to eat, these can be grilled outdoors or made in an oven. See photo opposite pg. 80.

Have ready:

8 oz. tempeh, steamed 15 minutes	1 large green pepper
1 pineapple or 1-14 oz. can pineapple chunks	1 sweet red pepper
	1 onion
	skewers*

Cut fresh pineapple into 1" chunks or drain canned pineapple.

In a sauce pan combine:

½ cup vegetable stock (or pineapple juice)	1 tsp. honey (omit if using pineapple juice)
2 Tbsp. tamari	1 inch gingerroot, chopped
2 Tbsp. lemon juice	1 Tbsp. arrowroot
1 tsp. dark sesame oil	

Simmer sauce a few minutes until thick and shiny. Cut tempeh in half crosswise, then into 1" squares. Add tempeh to sauce mixture, cover pan and simmer 5 minutes. Cool. Cut onions into chunks. Cut peppers into 1" squares. If desired, steam for 1 minute to soften, cool. Thread skewers, alternating squares of tempeh, peppers, onions and pineapple. If red peppers are not available, use cherry tomatoes for color.

Brush lightly with:
    1 Tbsp. oil

Place on grill and cook about 5 minutes on each side, or place in a broiling pan and cook about 5 inches from the source of heat, turning once, brushing with any leftover marinade.

*If using bamboo skewers, soak them for 30 minutes in cold water to prevent burning.

Per kebab: Calories: 60, Protein: 3 gm., Carbohydrates: 8 gm., Fat: 3 gm.

Brown Rice, Nut and Tempeh Casserole

Yield: 6 servings

This is good enough to serve with pride for Thanksgiving Day dinner.

Cut in half and place in sauce pan:
   8 oz. tempeh

Add, cover and simmer together for 10 minutes:
   1 bay leaf
   1 cup vegetable stock

Cool tempeh, remove bay leaf, reserve liquid.

Cook until rice is tender, about 40 minutes:
   1 cup brown rice, rinsed
   2 cups vegetable stock

Grate, crumble or cut small tempeh and combine with:
   2 Tbsp. tamari   **1 tsp. thyme**
   1 tsp. marjoram   **1 tsp. garlic powder**

Heat a skillet and sauté for 10 minutes:
   2 Tbsp. olive oil
   1 large onion, chopped
   1 cup celery, chopped

Add the tempeh and cook a few minutes more. Mix:
   the cooked rice   **¼ cup parsley, minced**
   sauteed onions, celery and **leftover liquid from cook-**
   **   tempeh**   **   ing tempeh**
   ¾ cup pecans, chopped

Spoon into a lightly oiled baking dish. Cover and bake at 350° for 15 minutes, remove cover and bake 15 minutes more. If casserole is made ahead, keep covered and chilled. Bake for 30 minutes covered to thoroughly cook. Serve with Brown Gravy or Mushroom Sauce.

Per serving: Calories: 285, Protein: 11 gm., Carbohydrates: 20 gm., Fat: 7 gm.

Brown Gravy

Yield: 2½ cups

In a dry sauce pan over medium low heat, cook, stirring occasionally until it begins to turn brown and you can smell it:
> ¼ **cup flour**

Stir into flour:
> **2 Tbsp. nutritional yeast**
> **¼ cup sunflower oil**

Cook and stir a few minutes, then add:
> **2 cups vegetable stock**
> **1 Tbsp. tamari**

Cook, stirring, until sauce thickens and bubbles.

Per ¼ cup serving: Calories: 64, Protein: ½ gm., Carbohydrates: 3 gm., Fat: 6 gm.

Mushroom Sauce

Yield: 3½ cups

Rinse, wipe clean:
> **6 oz. mushrooms**

Slice mushrooms. Heat in a skillet:
> **3 Tbsp. oil or margarine**

Cook mushrooms over medium high heat, stirring often, 7-8 minutes until browned. Sprinkle with:
> **3 Tbsp. flour**

Stir flour and mushrooms together, pour in:
> **2 cups vegetable stock**

Cook and stir until sauce is thickened. Taste for seasonings and add a little tamari or salt if needed. Remove from heat and stir in:
> **⅓ cup sour cream at room temperature**
> **a pinch of mace**

Return to heat and stir for 30 seconds.

Per ¼ cup serving: Calories: 47, Protein: 1 gm., Carbohydrates: 2 gm., Fat: 4 gm.

Firehouse Chili with Beans and Tempeh

Yield: 6 servings

Flavors develop if you make this ahead and reheat it.

Have ready:
>8 oz. tempeh, steamed for 10 minutes
>28 oz. can plum tomatoes, coarsely chopped
>20 oz. can red kidney beans with liquid

Heat a large heavy kettle and add:
>2 Tbsp. oil

Sauté until soft:
>1 large onion, chopped   1 green pepper, chopped
>2 cloves garlic, chopped

Grate or crumble the tempeh and add to the skillet. Sprinkle with:
>2 Tbsp. chili powder   1 tsp. basil
>1 tsp. coriander   2 Tbsp. tamari
>2 tsp. cumin   ¼ tsp. cayenne pepper

Cook and stir for 5-10 minutes to brown tempeh. Add canned tomatoes, bring to a boil and simmer for 15 minutes. Add kidney beans, with liquid, to kettle and simmer for 15 minutes.

Per serving: Calories: 245, Protein: 15 gm., Carbohydrates: 26 gm., Fat: 8 gm.

Chili Pie with Cornbread Topping

Yield: 8 servings

Pour two quarts of chili into a 9″ X 13″ baking dish. Preheat oven to 400°.

Mix together:
>8 oz. package corn muffin mix
>⅔ cup water or soymilk

Drop spoonfuls of mix on top of chili and bake for 20 minutes or until chili bubbles and cornbread is lightly browned.

Per serving: Calories: 306, Protein: 13 gm., Carbohydrates: 40 gm., Fat: 10 gm.

Walnut Tempeh Balls

Yield: 6 servings

These can be made ahead to delight dinner guests.

Steam for 15 minutes and set aside to cool:
    8 oz. tempeh

Heat in a sauce pan:
    2 Tbsp. oil

Add and cook until soft:
    ½ cup onion, chopped

Stir in:
    2 Tbsp. flour
    2 cups vegetable stock

Cook until thick and bubbly.

Put half of sauce in a bowl. Add:
2 Tbsp. parsley, minced	**½ tsp. marjoram**
½ tsp. thyme	**½ tsp. salt**

Grate the tempeh and add to bowl with:
    ½ cup fine soft bread crumbs
    ¾ cup walnuts, coarsely chopped in blender

Mix together, then shape into balls the size of a large walnut. Place in a lightly oiled baking dish.

Add to remaining sauce:
    2 Tbsp. parmesan cheese

Put a spoonful of sauce on top of each ball. Sprinkle with a dash of:
    paprika

Bake at 350° for 20 minutes. If made ahead and refrigerated, bring to room temperature before baking or bake a little longer.

Per serving: Calories: 342, Protein: 16 gm., Carbohydrates: 19 gm., Fat: 20 gm.

Tip   Bread crumbs can be made quickly by tearing up 1 slice of bread and whizzing in the blender.

Holiday Stuffing Casserole

Yield: 3 quarts

A marvelous dish with apples and pecans that can be made the day before the feast.

Cut about 12 slices of day old bread into half inch cubes, making:
> **8 cups bread cubes**

Heat oven to 300°, spread bread on a cookie sheet and bake about 15 minutes to dry out but not brown.

At the same time roast:
> **½ cup pecans, chopped**

Simmer for 15 minutes:
> **8 oz. tempeh, cut in half**
> **1 bay leaf**
> **1 cup vegetable stock**

Cool tempeh and cut into small dice. Sprinkle tempeh with:
> **2 Tbsp. tamari**

Lightly brown tempeh in a hot skillet with:
> **2 Tbsp. oil**

Have ready:
> **1 cup onions, chopped**
> **1 cup celery, chopped**
> **2 large, tart apples, peeled and chopped**

Heat a large skillet and add:
> **2 Tbsp. oil**

Sauté the onions about 5 minutes until softened, add the celery and apples, cook 5 minutes, then cover pan and cook 5 minutes more.

In a large bowl, mix together:

the bread cubes	**½ tsp. each of sage, thyme,**
the fried tempeh	**marjoram and mace**
onion, celery and apples	**¼ cup parsley, minced**
the roasted pecans	

Pour over mixture:
> **1½ cups vegetable stock:**

When well mixed, pack stuffing into a large, lightly oiled baking dish. Heat oven to 350°, cover pan with foil and bake for 30 minutes. uncover and bake for 15 minutes more. Good served with Brown Gravy, pg. 73.

Per 1 cup serving: Calories: 395, Protein: 13 gm., Carbohydrates: 56 gm., Fat: 10 gm.

Tempeh Loaf

Yield: 6 servings

Leftover loaf is delicious served cold in sandwiches.

Cut in half and place in a small saucepan:
8 oz. tempeh
1 cup vegetable stock
1 bay leaf

Cover and simmer for 10 minutes. Remove tempeh, cool and grate.

Pour hot stock over:
2 cups soft bread cubes, packed

Let bread soak while sautéing together:
2 Tbsp. olive oil
1 large onion, chopped small

Grate the tempeh, mix with the bread and fried onions and:
¼ cup parsley, minced   **½ tsp. oregano**
1 Tbsp. tamari or ½ tsp.   **½ tsp. thyme**
     salt   **2 Tbsp. Dijon mustard**
½ tsp. marjoram

Pack mixture into a lightly oiled loaf pan. Cover with foil and bake at 350° for 30 minutes.

Remove foil and place on top of loaf:
4 oz. mushrooms, sliced

Dot mushrooms with:
2 Tbsp. margarine

Bake 15 minutes more uncovered. Let loaf cool 10 minutes before slicing.

Per serving: Calories: 299, Protein: 13 gm., Carbohydrates: 30 gm., Fat: 7 gm.

Stuffed Savoy Cabbage

Yield: 6 servings

Tantalizing kitchen aromas as this old world specialty simmers on the stove on a cold winter day. See photo opposite pg. 65.

Wash well, discarding tough outer leaves:
1 large head Savoy cabbage

Set cabbage stem down in a colander in the sink and while gently separating the leaves, gradually pour over it:
4 qts. boiling water

Turn cabbage upside down to drain while preparing stuffing.

Mix in a bowl:

8 oz. tempeh, steamed, cooled, grated	**½ tsp. garlic powder**
1 medium onion, chopped	**½ tsp. thyme**
¼ cup parsley, minced	**½ tsp. marjoram**
½ cup toasted bread crumbs	**½ tsp. oregano**
	1 tsp. salt or 2 Tbsp. tamari

Arrange 3 pieces of string on counter top, set cabbage on strings. Gently insert stuffing between the leaves. Close the cabbage, tying with strings.

Tuck under top of string:
1 bay leaf

Place in a large cooking pan that has a tight cover:
2 Tbsp. olive oil

Arrange vegetables in kettle:
6 carrots, cut in half
3 onions, cut in half

Place cabbage on vegetables. Pour over:
1 cup warm vegetable stock:

If there is room in pan, add 6 scrubbed potatoes. Cover pan tightly, bring to a boil, then reduce heat to low and simmer 45 minutes. Or heat oven to 350° and bake 45 minutes. Check after 20 minutes to make sure there is enough liquid so it doesn't cook dry. When vegetables are tender, lift out cabbage and set on a warm platter.

Remove strings and bay leaf. Surround with cooked carrots and onions. Cooking juices can be poured over cabbage, Cut into wedges to serve.

Per serving: Calories: 243, Protein: 15 gm., Carbohydrates: 29 gm., Fat: 5 gm.

Cajun Dirty Beans and Rice

Yield: 6 servings

A New Orleans favorite with tempeh added.

Have ready:
> 2½ cups cooked rice (1 cup raw)
> 2 cups cooked pinto or red beans
> 8 oz. tempeh, simmered in 1 cup stock 10 minutes

Sauté over medium heat about 5 minutes:
> 2 Tbsp. olive oil
> 1 cup onions, chopped
> 1 green pepper, chopped

Add and cook a few minutes more:
> 2 cloves garlic, chopped
> ½ cup celery, chopped

Add the cooked vegetables to the rice. Cut the tempeh into small dice and mix with:
> 1 Tbsp. chili powder
> 1 Tbsp. tamari

Heat skillet and add:
> 2 Tbsp. oil

Sauté the seasoned tempeh over medium high heat until lightly browned.

Mix together in a large bowl:
> the cooked rice   1 Tbsp. chili powder
> the vegetables   1 tsp. cumin
> the cooked beans

Stir the tempeh into the mixture, then pile into a large, lightly oiled baking dish. Cover dish and bake at 350° about 25 minutes.

Per serving: Calories: 342, Protein: 15 gm., Carbohydrates: 40 gm., Fat: 6 gm.

Chili Dog Rolls

Yield: 20 rolls

A treat for summer picnics and backpack lunches. If you're lucky enough to have any leftover, they freeze well and can be reheated.

Simmer for 10 minutes, then set aside to cool:

8 oz. tempeh **1 cup vegetable stock**

Make a dough by dissolving:

1 Tbsp. dry yeast **1 Tbsp. honey**
¼ cup warm water

Stir in:

2 Tbsp. oil **5 to 6 cups flour, half**
1 cup warm water **unbleached white, half**
½ tsp. salt **whole wheat**

When dough is hard to stir, work with your hands, kneading in enough flour to make a dough that is not too sticky to handle. Knead about 5 minutes. put a few drops of oil in a large, clean bowl, roll the ball of dough around to coat, then cover with a towel and put in a warm place to rise double.

While dough rises, make the filling. Sauté together:

2 Tbsp. olive oil **1 green pepper, chopped**
1 cup onions, chopped

Grate or crumble the tempeh and mix with:

2 Tbsp. tamari **1 tsp. garlic powder**
1 Tbsp. chili powder **1 tsp. oregano**
1 tsp. cumin

Remove onions and peppers to a bowl, heat skillet and:

2 Tbsp. oil

Add the seasoned tempeh and fry, stirring occasionally, about 10 minutes. Add tempeh to onions and stir in:

6 oz. can tomato paste

Taste mixture and add a little salt, if desired, or a little cayenne if you like it hotter.

When dough has risen, punch down and divide into 4 balls. Lightly oil 2 baking sheets. On a lightly floured work surface, roll each ball out into a long oblong about 25" X 5". Cut dough evenly into 5 pieces. Place ¼ cup of filling between one edge and the center of

each piece, leaving some free edges of dough. Roll up tightly, pinching ends and place seam side down on baking sheets. Continue until all dough and filling is used (20 rolls). Let rise 20 minutes. Preheat oven to 375° and bake for 20-25 minutes until lightly browned. Transfer to rack to cool. Serve hot or cold, with mustard if desired.

Per roll: Calories: 174, Protein: 6 gm., Carbohydrates: 25 gm., Fat: 5 gm.

Stuffed Glazed Acorn Squash

Yield: 4 servings

A winter vegetable becomes a main dish with the addition of tempeh for protein and substance.

Split in half and scoop out seeds and membrane from:
   2 medium acorn squash

Place flesh side down in a baking dish and add:
   ½ cup water

Bake at 350° about 20 minutes while preparing filling.

Simmer for 15 minutes:
   6 oz. tempeh   **½ cup water**
   1 bay leaf

Cool, drain tempeh and crumble or grate. Sauté in a hot skillet:
   2 Tbsp. olive oil   **½ cup celery, chopped**
   1 medium onion, chopped

Add tempeh to skillet and season with:
   ½ tsp. each thyme, marjoram and oregano
   1 Tbsp. tamari

Cook a few minutes. Stir into mixture:
   ½ cup breadcrumbs   **⅓ cup walnuts, chopped (opt.)**

Turn squash up and fill cavities with stuffing.

For a glaze, mix:
   1 Tbsp. maple syrup or honey
   1 tsp. lemon juice

Brush edges of squash with glaze. Place in lightly oiled baking dish and bake at 350° about 30 minutes, until squash is fork tender.

Per serving: Calories: 355, Protein: 13 gm., Carbohydrates: 50 gm., Fat: 6 gm.

Four Star Mince Pie, pg. 93

Sausage Patties

Yield: 12 patties

A breakfast treat, delicious in a biscuit or with pancakes.

Cook for 10 minutes:
8 oz. tempeh, cut in half   ½ cup vegetable stock

Cool tempeh, grate on coarse side of grater. Mix with:
**¼ cup rolled oats   1 Tbsp. oil
2 Tbsp. tamari   1 tsp. each of sage, thyme,
2 Tbsp. water   marjoram**

Mixture should be moist enough to press into 12 patties. Chill on a covered platter.

Heat a large skillet and add:
2 Tbsp. oil

Brown patties on each side over medium high heat, turning carefully. You may want to do this in small batches, using just a little oil each time. Patties will soak up the oil quickly but will brown in the dry pan.

Per patty: Calories: 75, Protein: 4 gm., Carbohydrates: 3 gm., Fat: 5 gm.

Potato Sausage Patties

Yield: 16 patties

A treat that children will love.

Have ready:
4 cups mashed potatoes

Cook for 20 minutes:
8 oz. tempeh   1 cup vegetable stock

Cool and grate the tempeh. Mix it with:
**1 Tbsp. tamari   1 tsp. marjoram
1 tsp. thyme   ½ tsp. sage**

Sauté until onion is soft:
**2 Tbsp. oil
½ cup onion, chopped**

Mix together the cooled mashed potatoes, the tempeh and the onion.

If desired, add:
 ¼ cup parsley, minced

Shape mixture into 16 patties. Patties can be made ahead and chilled on a covered plate.

Heat a large skillet and:
 2 Tbsp. oil

Fry the patties until brown on both sides, lifting carefully with a pancake turner while turning so as not to break up the crust that forms.

Per patty: Calories: 97, Protein: 4 gm., Carbohydrates: 8 gm., Fat: 5 gm.

Apple Cider Baked Tempeh

Yield: 4 servings

A simple dish that will appeal to children as well as adults.

Have ready:
 8 oz. tempeh   **1 cup apple cider**

Cut defrosted tempeh in half crosswise, then cut each thin slab into 4 pieces. Score with shallow diagonal slashes. Place in a bowl and pour cider over tempeh. Cover and marinate at least an hour in refrigerator, turning over once or twice. Drain, save juice.

Dredge tempeh slices in mixture of:
 ¼ cup flour   **½ tsp. salt**
 ½ tsp. ground ginger **½ tsp. paprika**

Heat in a skillet:
 2 Tbsp. oil

Quickly brown slices and place in a baking dish. Top with:
 2 Granny Smith apples, sliced

Heat remaining cider and stir in:
 2 tsp. honey

Pour liquid over apples and tempeh and sprinkle top with:
 ½ tsp. cinnamon

Cover pan and bake at 350° for 30-40 minutes, until apples are tender. Uncover for last 10 minutes of baking.

Per serving: Calories: 286, Protein: 12 gm., Carbohydrates: 30 gm., Fat: 12 gm.

Stuffed Vegetables

Yield: 6 servings

Make the most of summer's bounty of vegetables by stuffing an assortment. Eggplant, peppers, mushrooms, tomatoes and zucchini are all good. Vary the seasonings and use fresh herbs if possible.

Stuffed Peppers:
Use **6 small peppers** (about 3" high), removing tops and seeds, or use 3 large peppers, cutting in half lengthwise. Parboil shells 2 minutes, drain and cool.

Sauté about 5 minutes:
> **2 Tbsp. olive oil**
> **1 medium onion, chopped**

Steam for 10 minutes, cool and grate:
> **4 oz. tempeh**

Stir into the tempeh:
> **½ tsp. each oregano, marjoram, garlic powder and salt**

Mix together the onions, tempeh and:
> **1 cup cold cooked rice (or bulghur, couscous or kasha)**
> **½ cup tomatoes, chopped**
> **2 Tbsp. parsley, minced**

Stuff the shells, place in a lightly oiled baking pan, cover with foil and bake at 375° about 30 minutes.

Per stuffed pepper: Calories: 131, Protein: 6 gm., Carbohydrates: 13 gm., Fat: 3 gm.

Stuffed Zucchini:
Choose **6 young, small zucchini**, about 4" long. Cut in half lengthwise and with a grapefruit knife scoop out pulp, leaving a shell about ¼" thick. Steam shells and proceed as above, omitting the rice or other grain as pulp gives you bulk.

Instead of oregano, marjoram and parsley use:
> **¼ cup mint leaves, chopped**　　**1 tsp. coriander**
> **1 tsp. cumin**　　**½ tsp. salt**
> 　　**dash of cayenne**

Stuff shells, cover and bake as above.

Sauerbraten

Yield: 6 servings

Flavors of the marinade soak into the tempeh and make a delectable gravy.

Cut in half crosswise, so there are 2 thin slabs:
8 oz. tempeh

Cut tempeh into 1-inch squares. Place in bowl with marinade made of:

1 cup apple cider or juice	**2 Tbsp. catsup**
1 cup water	**2 Tbsp. vinegar**
3 whole allspice	**1 Tbsp. Worchestershire**
2 cloves garlic, cut in half	**sauce**
1 bay leaf	**1 tsp. powdered ginger**

Let the tempeh soak several hours. Remove tempeh with slotted spoon, reserving marinade for sauce.

Heat a skillet with:
2 Tbsp. oil

Quickly brown the tempeh pieces, placing into a casserole. Stir into the reserved marinade:
2 Tbsp. arrowroot

Cook the sauce in a small saucepan until it is thickened, pour over tempeh. Cover and bake at 350° for 20 minutes. If made ahead and casserole is cold, bake a little longer until sauce is bubbly. Serve with brown rice or cooked noodles.

Per serving: Calories: 150, Protein: 8 gm., Carbohydrates: 10 gm., Fat: 8 gm.

Strogonoff with Mushrooms in Creamy Gravy

Yield: 6 servings

This is a recipe I'd recommend for someone new to tempeh as the flavors are delightful.

Simmer for 15 minutes:
>**8 oz. tempeh, cut in half**   **1 bay leaf**
>**1 cup water**

Cool. Cut into thin slices about 2" long. Sprinkle with:
>**2 Tbsp. tamari**

Let stand while preparing mushrooms and sauce. Rinse and wipe dry:
>**8 oz. mushrooms**

Slice mushrooms. heat a skillet with:
>**1 Tbsp. oil**

Add the mushrooms and sauté quickly over medium high heat until they begin to brown and give out their juices. Place in a bowl.

Heat skillet and add:
>**2 Tbsp. oil**   **the drained tempeh pieces**

Quickly brown the tempeh and remove to bowl with mushrooms.

Heat skillet and add:
>**1 Tbsp. oil**   **1 cup onions, chopped**

Cook until onions are soft. Sprinkle onions with:
>**2 Tbsp. arrowroot**

Stir in slowly:
>**2 cups hot vegetable stock**

Cook sauce about 5 minutes until it thickens and bubbles, then reduce heat and slowly stir in:
>**½ cup sour cream, at room temperature**

Add the mushrooms and tempeh to the pan to heat through, being careful not to boil the sauce. Serve over cooked noodles.

Per serving: Calories: 236, Protein: 10 gm., Carbohydrates: 10 gm., Fat: 16 gm.

Hungarian Paprikash

Yield: 6 servings

Keep paprika in the refrigerator to retain its color and flavor.

Simmer for 15 minutes in a covered pan:
> **8 oz. tempeh, cut in half**
> **1 cup vegetable stock**
> **1 bay leaf**

Cool the tempeh and cut into thin slices, 2" long. Heat a skillet and add:
> **2 Tbsp. oil**

Fry the tempeh until lightly browned, sprinkling with:
> **1 Tbsp. tamari**

Sauté until onion is soft:
> **½ cup onion, chopped**
> **½ cup green pepper, chopped**

Add:
> **1 clove garlic, minced**
> **8 oz. mushrooms, thinly sliced**

Cook mushrooms 3 to 4 minutes, sprinkle with:
> **2 Tbsp. flour**

Stir and cook 3 minutes. Add:
> **4 tsp. Hungarian paprika**

Cook for 1 minute. Stir in:
> **2 Tbsp. tomato paste**
> **1 Tbsp. lemon juice**
> **1 cup vegetable stock**

Mix well. Remove from heat and stir in:
> **⅔ cup sour cream*, at room temperature**

Heat the sauce, but do not let it boil. Stir in the tempeh. Serve over hot cooked noodles.

*For a less rich dish, use yogurt instead of sour cream.

Per serving: Calories: 198, Protein: 10 gm., Carbohydrates: 8 gm., Fat: 12 gm.

Strudel Roll with Tempeh Filling

Yield: 6 servings

A tasty filling rolled up in flaky filo leaves that can be made ahead and baked before serving.

Have ready:
> **half of a 1 lb. pkg. filo dough**

Filo dough is available frozen at supermarkets. A pound package has about 20 sheets of the thin strudel dough. Defrost package overnight in refrigerator. Remove half the sheets from the package for this recipe, then replace remaining sheets in the original plastic and box and freeze for later use. Have filling, bread crumbs and melted garlic margarine ready before you take out the filo sheets. Work quickly before filo dries out. Torn sheets can be used.

Simmer for 15 minutes:
> **8 oz. tempeh**　　　　　　**1 bay leaf**
> **1 cup vegetable broth**

Set aside to cool and grate. Heat a skillet and sauté:
> **2 Tbsp. olive oil**　　　　**2 chopped garlic cloves**
> **½ cup onion, chopped**

In a mixing bowl combine:
> **the grated tempeh**　　　　**¼ cup parsley, chopped**
> **cooked onions and garlic**　**½ tsp. each thyme, mar-**
> **1 large carrot, grated**　　　**joram and salt**

Have ready:
> **¼ cup margarine, melted with**
> **3 cloves garlic, put through press and mixed with**
> **1 Tbsp. olive oil**

Also have ready:
> **¾ cup fine bread crumbs**

Unroll filo leaves, place one flat on work counter and quickly brush with a little garlic margarine, using a pastry brush or finger tips. Repeat with a second sheet on top of the first and sprinkle with some of the breadcrumbs. Sprinkle half the tempeh filling on the third sheet. Add another sheet, brush with margarine, then another with margarine and crumbs, then sprinkle on remaining filling. Top with remaining sheets, with margarine and crumbs between them. Roll up sheets like a jelly roll into a long oblong. Rub top with last of garlic margarine. Lift carefully onto a cookie sheet at a diagonal so it will fit. Slice through the loaf with a sharp knife, almost to the bottom leaf, into 12 slices. Bake in a preheated oven at 375° for 20-25 minutes until lightly browned. This is good served with Brown Gravy or Mushroom Sauce (pg. 73).

Per serving: Calories: 402, Protein: 12 gm., Carbohydrates: 28 gm., Fat: 13 gm.

Couscous Pilaf with Pine Nuts

Yield: 6 servings

Toasting pignolia, the seeds from certain pine cones, brings out their full flavor.

Simmer together for 15 minutes:

8 oz. tempeh   **1 bay leaf**
1 cup vegetable stock

Cool. Heat a 2-quart pan and cook, stirring for 2 minutes to coat the grains:

2 Tbsp. olive oil   **1½ cups couscous**

Pour in:

2 cups hot vegetable stock

Cook 1-2 minutes, fluffing with a fork, until liquid is absorbed. Remove from heat, cover and keep warm.

Heat a skillet and sauté:

1 Tbsp. olive oil   **½ cup pine nuts (pignola)**

Cook nuts 1-2 minutes, add:

½ cup onions, chopped   **1 red pepper, chopped**
½ cup celery, chopped

When onions are soft, stir the vegetables and pine nuts into the couscous.

Heat skillet and sauté steamed tempeh, diced small, in:

2 Tbsp. olive oil

When tempeh is browned, add to couscous with:

2 Tbsp. lemon juice   **¼ cup currants**

Taste and add a little salt if desired.

Per serving: Calories: 365, Protein: 11 gm., Carbohydrates: 23 gm., Fat: 13 gm.

Moussaka

Eggplant in an exotic dish from Greece and the Middle-East.

Peel and slice into ½″ thick slices:
> **2 medium eggplants (1½ lbs.)**

Layer in a bowl and sprinkle salt over the layers to remove the bitterness. Fill with cold water to cover and weight down the eggplant with a plate. Leave to soak for 30 minutes.

Simmer for 10 minutes:
> **8 oz. tempeh**   **1 bay leaf**
> **1 cup vegetable stock**

Set aside to cool.

In a quart saucepan sauté:
> **2 Tbsp. olive oil**   **1 cup tomatoes, chopped**
> **1 cup onions, chopped**

When onions are nearly soft, add:
> **½ cup breadcrumbs**   **¼ tsp. nutmeg**
> **½ tsp. basil**

Set aside. Prepare topping by making a white sauce. Combine in a small saucepan:
> **¼ cup flour**   **1½ cups vegetable stock**
> **2 Tbsp. oil**

Stir over medium heat until thick. Stir in:
> **¼ cup parmesan cheese, grated or ¼ cup plain yogurt**

Blend in a blender until smooth and add to the sauce:
> **¼ lb. tofu**

Drain eggplant and rinse with cold water to remove the salt.

In a large skillet fry until browned:
> **1 Tbsp. olive oil**
> **½ the drained eggplant slices**

The slices will absorb the oil quickly but will continue to brown. You can arrange the smaller slices along the sides of the pan until the larger slices are done and can be removed.

Arrange the browned slices in the bottom of an oiled 8″ X 8″ pan. Crumble over half the simmered tempeh. Spread on half the onion and tomato mixture. Repeat the process, frying the remaining eggplant slices and layering them with the rest of the tempeh, crumbled, and the onions and tomatoes. Press the layers down into the pan with the back of a spoon and top with the sauce. Bake in a 350° oven for 25 minutes. Allow to cool 15 minutes before slicing and serving. If made ahead, cover with foil and refrigerate until baking time, then cook a little longer until filling just begins to bubble.

Per serving: Calories: 334, Protein: 15 gm., Carbohydrates: 24 gm., Fat: 7 gm.

Indonesian Satay

Yield: 6 servings

Ground candlenuts are used in Indonesia for this spicy sauce, but peanuts work as well. The marinated tempeh can be served in slices or cut smaller and threaded on skewers to grill.

Whiz in a blender:
½ cup roasted peanuts

Add to blender:

1 small onion	**½ tsp. tumeric**
1 clove garlic	**¼ tsp. red chili pepper**
1″ gingerroot, cut up	**flakes**
2 Tbsp. tamari	**juice of half a lemon**

Blend, adding gradually:
1 cup water

If you like it hot, add a little more of the red crushed pepper flakes. Pour into the top of a double boiler, place over boiling water and cook sauce 20 minutes, stirring occasionally. Or put into a 1-quart measure, cover with plastic wrap and cook 3 to 5 minutes in a microwave on high.

Simmer for 20 minutes:
8 oz. tempeh
1 cup vegetable stock

Cool, slice thinly and soak in satay sauce for several hours or overnight. Just before serving, fry slices in a little oil or grill under a broiler. Or cut tempeh into thin strips, thread onto skewers, brush with marinade and a little olive oil and cook on a grill.

Per serving: Calories: 157, Protein: 11 gm., Carbohydrates: 7 gm., Fat: 6 gm.

Curried Tempeh with Apple

Yield: 6 servings

Tantalizing aroma and flavors in this Indian feast dish.

Defrost, cut into half inch cubes:
> **8 oz. tempeh**

Place in a saucepan with:
> **2 cups vegetable stock**

Cover pan and simmer 15 minutes. Cool and drain tempeh, reserving broth.

Heat a skillet and add:
> **2 Tbsp. oil**

Sauté until soft:
> **1 medium onion, chopped**

Add:
> **1 large tart apple, chopped**

Cook 5 minutes more. Sprinkle with:
> **1 or 2 Tbsp. curry powder***   **½ tsp. garlic powder**
> **2 Tbsp. arrowroot**   **½ tsp. honey**
> **½ tsp. mace**

*Depending on how hot you like it.

Cook 3 minutes. Measure broth remaining from tempeh and add enough water to make 2 cups of liquid. Slowly stir liquid into onions, stir and cook until thickened and bubbly. Add:
> **¼ cup currants or raisins**

Set pan over hot water, cover and cook 30 minutes to blend flavors, stirring occasionally. Sauce can be refrigerated overnight.

Cut the steamed tempeh into small cubes, brown cubes in:
> **2 Tbsp. oil**

Add tempeh to curry sauce just before serving. Serve with brown rice and an assortment of condiments such as: coconut, chopped green onions, raisins, chopped peanuts, yogurt and chutney.

Per serving: Calories: 214, Protein: 8 gm., Carbohydrates: 15 gm., Fat: 13 gm.

DESSERT

Four Star Mince Pie

Yield: 8 servings

A delicious dessert that can be made with organic dried apples or with fresh. See photo opposite pg. 81.

Soak in a covered dish overnight:
2 cups dried sliced apples   **1 cup hot water**

Simmer together for 10 minutes:
8 oz. tempeh, cut in half   **½ cup apple cider or juice**

Do not drain apples or tempeh.

Make a pie crust by mixing:
2 cups whole wheat pastry flour
⅓ to ½ cup of oil
¼ cup cold water

Stir into a ball, adding a few drops more water if necessary. Divide into two balls, roll out into circles 2 inches larger than your 9 " pie pan. Fit bottom crust into pan.

Cool tempeh, grate on coarse side of grater.

In a bowl, mix the soaked apples and grated tempeh (with any liquid remaining). Add:

½ cup raisins   **1 tsp. cinnamon**
½ cup chopped walnuts   **1 tsp. nutmeg**
2 Tbsp. honey   **½ tsp. allspice**
1 Tbsp. oil   **½ tsp. mace**
1 tsp. finely shredded **½ tsp. salt**
** lemon peel**

Pile mixture into bottom of 9" crust. Cover with top crust, seal and flute edges with a fork. Slash top in 4 or 6 places to allow steam to escape. Bake in a preheated oven at 425° for 15 minutes. Lower heat to 350° and bake 40-45 minutes more until lightly browned.

Per serving: Calories: 405, Protein: 12 gm., Carbohydrates: 45 gm., Fat: 20 gm.

Index

R

Red Lentil Soup, 31
Rice with Almonds, Mexican, 61
Ruebens en Croissant, 39

S

San Joaquin Salad, 21
Sandwich Loaf with Guacamole and
    Tempeh, 40
Sandwich Spread, Hummus and
    Tempeh, 42
Satay, Indonesian, 91
Sauerbraten, 85
Sausage Patties, 82
Sausage Patties, Potato, 82
Scallop with Shiitake Mushrooms,
    Potato Tomato, 53
Scallopine with Red and Green
    Peppers, 58
Shells Italiano, Mini, 57
shiitake mushrooms, 9
Shiitake Mushrooms and Garlic
    Sauce, 43
soymilk, 9
Spanish Sausage (Chorizo), 68
Spinach Mushroom Salad, 26
Split Pea Soup with Barley and
    Tempeh, 36
Spread with Capers and Onions, 19
Stir Fry with Ginger and Sesame,
    Cabbage, 49
storing tempeh, 7
Strogonoff with Mushrooms in
    Creamy Gravy, 86
Strudel Roll with Tempeh Filling, 88
Stuffed
    Avocado, 22
    Glazed Acorn Squash, 81
    Grape Leaves (Dolmas), 13
    Jumbo Shells, 59
    Savoy Cabbage, 78
    Vegetables, 84
Stuffing Casserole, Holiday, 76
Sukiyaki with Broccoli &
    Cauliflower, 45
Super Hero, 41
Sweet and Sour Tempeh, 47
Szechuan Tempeh with Almonds, 44

T

Taco Shells with Mexican Filling, 64
tamari, 9
tempeh
    culture, about, 6, 10-11
    starter, 10-11
    cooking, 7
    making, 10-11
    nutritive values for, 6
    storing, 7
Tempeh
    Balls, Walnut, 75
    Burgers, 38
    Casserole, Brown Rice, Nut and, 72
    Filling, Burritos with, 65
    Filling, Strudel Roll with, 88
    Loaf, 77
    on Rice Noodles, Mandarin, 48
    with Almonds, Szechuan, 44
    with Apple, Curried, 92
    Barbecued in Buns, 38
    Sweet and Sour, 47
Tetrazinni Turino, 56
Tidbits, Ginger Tamari, 20
Tomato Stars, 22
Tostadas with Corn Tortillas, 66
Tuna Salad, Mock, 22
Tuscany Two Bean Soup, 34
Two Bean Soup, Tuscany, 34

V

vegetable stock, 9
Vegetable Soup Provençale, 32
Vegetables, Stuffed, 84

W

Walnut Tempeh Balls, 75
Warm Red Cabbage Slaw, 27
White Bean and Potato Chowder, 34

Y

Yeast Sauce, Nutritional, 62
Yogurt Cheese, 61